T0110710

Cambridge Elements ≡

Elements in Publishing and Book Culture
edited by
Samantha Rayner
University College London
Leah Tether
University of Bristol

THE FRANKFURT BOOK FAIR AND BESTSELLER BUSINESS

Beth Driscoll
University of Melbourne

Claire Squires
University of Stirling

CAMBRIDGE
UNIVERSITY PRESS

CAMBRIDGE
UNIVERSITY PRESS

University Printing House, Cambridge CB2 8BS, United Kingdom

One Liberty Plaza, 20th Floor, New York, NY 10006, USA

477 Williamstown Road, Port Melbourne, VIC 3207, Australia

314–321, 3rd Floor, Plot 3, Splendor Forum, Jasola District Centre,
New Delhi – 110025, India

79 Anson Road, #06–04/06, Singapore 079906

Cambridge University Press is part of the University of Cambridge.

It furthers the University's mission by disseminating knowledge in the pursuit of
education, learning, and research at the highest international levels of excellence.

www.cambridge.org
Information on this title: www.cambridge.org/9781108928106
DOI: 10.1017/9781108933377

© Beth Driscoll and Claire Squires 2020

This publication is in copyright. Subject to statutory exception
and to the provisions of relevant collective licensing agreements,
no reproduction of any part may take place without the written
permission of Cambridge University Press.

First published 2020

A catalogue record for this publication is available from the British Library.

ISBN 978-1-108-92810-6 Paperback
ISSN 2514-8524 (online)
ISSN 2514-8516 (print)

Additional resources for this publication at www.cambridge.org/driscoll.

Cambridge University Press has no responsibility for the persistence or accuracy of
URLs for external or third-party internet websites referred to in this publication
and does not guarantee that any content on such websites is, or will remain,
accurate or appropriate.

The Frankfurt Book Fair and Bestseller Business

Elements in Publishing and Book Culture

DOI: 10.1017/9781108933377

First published online: September 2020

Beth Driscoll

University of Melbourne

Claire Squires

University of Stirling

Author for correspondence: Beth Driscoll, driscoll@unimelb.edu.au

ABSTRACT: The Frankfurt Book Fair is the leading global industry venue for rights sales, facilitating business-to-buzzness deals and international networks. In this Element, we pursue an Ullapoolist approach to excavate beneath the production of bestsellers at the Fair. Our investigation involved three consecutive years of fieldwork (2017-2019) including interviews and autoethnographic, arts-informed interventions. The Element argues that buzz at the Fair exists in two states: as market-ready media reports and partial, lived experiences linked to mood. The physical structures and absences of the Fair enact its power relations and direct the flow of books and buzz. Further, the Fair is not only a site for commercial exchange but a carnival of sorts, marked by disruptive historical events and problematic socio-political dynamics. Key themes emerging from the Element are the presence of excess, the pseudo(neo)liberal self-satisfaction of book culture, and the interplay of optimism and pessimism in contemporary publishing.

KEYWORDS: Frankfurt Book Fair, publishing, bestsellers, marketing, buzz, book cultures, Ullapoolism

© Beth Driscoll and Claire Squires

ISBNs: 9781108928106 (PB), 9781108933377 (OC)

ISSNs: 2514-8524 (online), 2514-8516 (print)

Contents

Introduction: Flight Paths

Imagine a paper plane loaded up with paper books and paper publishers. It's flying from Delhi to Frankfurt, or maybe from Tbilisi to Frankfurt, or perhaps from New York to Frankfurt. There are lots of paper planes. Some of them fly fast and far. Some of them get stuck in trees. Some of them converge at midway points, where paper publishers rush between gates to make connections, tapping on paper phones the moment they get Wi-Fi. At the paper airport in Frankfurt, the paper publishers collect their paper baggage and disperse to hotels, perhaps drinking a Negroni in the lobby before converging once again at the Frankfurt Book Fair.

Paper planes are fun to make and to fly. They also prompt reflection on the material activity undergirding a trade that can seem virtual, global and frictionless: the sale of international rights to book-based content. A great deal of physical movement, unequally distributed and routed via the central node of the Frankfurt Book Fair, is necessary to produce the key goods of the publishing industry – successful books.

***

This book (itself available as a paper element or as a digital one) is about the Frankfurt Book Fair and its role in the publishing of bestsellers. The Book Fair, or in its native German, Buchmesse, is presided over by the Frankfurter Buchmesse GmbH, a subsidiary of the Börsenverein des Deutschen Buchhandels Beteiligungsgesellschaft mbH (BBG), which was founded by the Börsenverein des deutschen Buchhandels (the German Publishers and Booksellers Association). The Fair is an international forum for the exchange of rights and a showcase for books and publishing. With its origins in the fifteenth century and a renewed role after World War II, the Buchmesse is where the industry gathers en masse once a year, often described as 'the largest of all' trade events in the global publishing industry (Owen 2019). It presents what we term 'megativity', a positive attitude expressed through physical scale and future-oriented behaviours, including the trading of rights. It is where new entrants to the industry go to establish an international presence, the place 'Everyone attends because everyone attends' (Niemeier 2001, 111). In 2019 the Buchmesse hosted 7,450 exhibitors, 302,267 visitors, 4,000 events and 10,000 journalists; while this confirms its size, the Fair is physically smaller than it used to be, occupying two fewer halls in the Messe complex than in 2015 (Frankfurter Buchmesse 2019a; Nawotka 2019a). This retraction notwithstanding, the Buchmesse still presents itself and is thought of as the key annual destination for global book business (or 'buzzness', as we have termed it), the most important date on the publishing calendar.

At a symbolic level 'Frankfurt' is a byword in the contemporary publishing industry. It is a term around which a host of associations, assumptions and values coalesce. Frankfurt is a semi-mythical placeholder that represents the centre of book publishing, and especially publishing's most high-profile products: bestsellers. It is also a focal point for much of the publishing industry's optimism and forward-looking energy, particularly important given, and intriguingly counterposed with, publishing's long-standing tendency to be powered by existential 'crisis' or 'apocalypse' (Taylor 1989, 1; Lewis-Kraus 2009) including anxieties about the decline of reading. Publishing is an industry that derives energy from its efforts to document, understand and even influence the sometimes hostile world which surrounds it. In this context bestsellers are proof that books still find readers and they provide the cash influx that supports other books. The Frankfurt Book Fair is an event explicitly oriented around hope: what might sell, where and in what format.

The Buchmesse lasts for only a few days each October, but it is widely discussed in the media in the lead-up to the Fair and for months afterwards as the industry and the public try to grasp the shape of book culture, especially through its key trends. Industry newsletters and websites present insider accounts of the Fair; trade associations feature news about Frankfurt on their websites for the benefit of members.[1] The books sections of newspapers such as *The Guardian* or the *New York Times* often refer to Frankfurt amongst their reviews and articles. News of Frankfurt reaches

---

[1] Industry newsletters include *The Bookseller* (UK), *Publishers Weekly* (USA), *Books+Publishing* (Australia), *Livres Hebdo* (France) and *Boersenblatt* (Germany). For examples of industry association reports see Australian Publishers Association (2018) and Publishing Scotland (2019).

a broader audience through cultural journalism, such as the long-form articles we discuss in Chapter 3. And a potential bestseller will often be introduced to booksellers with an account of its success at Frankfurt. In these narratives a particular vocabulary is used to write about Frankfurt and future bestsellers. Books are snapped up in bidding wars. Books are sensations. Books are hot property.

There is a gap, though, between how the Fair is reported and how it is experienced. Much more happens at Frankfurt than rights sales of hot books. The layout of the Fair includes thousands of exhibitors from across the world who exhibit on stands grouped by linguistic, cultural and geo-political affinities. The *Ehrengast*, or guest of honour designation, introduced in 1976, showcases the literature and culture of a country (or sometimes region or language group) through a dedicated, decorative pavilion at the Messe and a series of programmes and events. Opening ceremonies and author talks celebrate freedom of speech, even as political unrest sporadically punctures the veneer of liberal discourse. In addition to these political dimensions of the Fair, social dynamics intersect with its economic activity. Exhibitors, visitors and journalists talk and network at meetings, in the halls and at nearby hotels and restaurants. The production of an international bestseller sits on top of layer after layer of Buchmesse activity. How then can researchers best approach this complex, pivotal site of contemporary book culture?

Ullapoolism

This book enacts and develops an Ullapoolist research approach. Ullapoolism is a programme of playful, material, satirical and sociable research producing situated knowledge and creative critique and using arts-informed methods.[2] It is informed by previous models for the study of book culture, including Robert Darnton's communications circuit of the book (1982), Pierre Bourdieu's field of literary production (1993) and Pascale Casanova's *World Republic of Letters* (2004), but breaks with these in order to engage more comprehensively with the nowness of contemporary culture. As outlined in our article 'The Epistemology of Ullapoolism: Making Mischief from within Contemporary Book Culture'

---

[2] For more information visit https://ullapoolism.wordpress.com/.

(Driscoll and Squires 2020b), Ullapoolism is a sensing-thinking-doing epistemology, an interventionist conceptual and activist art practice.

Ullapoolism draws inspiration from the Situationist International's opposition to commodity capitalism and the 'spectacle' which renders people as passive consumers (Debord (1967) 2014). Two of the situationists' key modes are the détournement, a parodic rewriting of images and texts, and the dérive, a practice of actively drifting through urban environments and responding to the emotions they inspire. Our own détournements to date have included card and board games that investigate the dynamics of literary festivals, pyjamas that reflect upon the materiality of reading in a post-digital age and a spot-the-difference quiz that plays on the similar-sounding names of musician and actor Janelle Monáe and author Gerald Murnane; our dérives have included the thoughtful drowning of a copy of *Moby Dick* to further our explorations of boats and books (Driscoll and Squires 2018a, 2018b, 2018c).

As explained further in Chapter 2, Ullapoolism also finds inspiration in 'low theory', a term proposed by Stuart Hall and adapted by Jack Halberstam in *The Queer Art of Failure* (2011). Low theory is a 'kind of theoretical model that flies under the radar' and 'tries to locate all the in-between spaces' (Halberstam 2011, 16 and 2). It is attuned to 'the small, the inconsequential, the antimonumental, the micro, the irrelevant' and chases 'whims and fantasies' (Halberstam 2011, 21), a mode we adopt in order to advance our cultural analysis and scholarly activism.

Because Ullapoolism is interventionist, researching from within publishing networks is integral to our work. We are not disinterested observers, but active players and sometimes instigators of the situations of contemporary book cultures. In this book we pursue this approach to argue that the Fair is a layered site where the economic activity of any given year occurs in tandem with enduring geopolitical and social inequities, along with political, cultural and environmental challenges. This approach significantly extends earlier scholarship on the Frankfurt Book Fair and on the publishing of bestsellers.

Scholarship on the Frankfurt Book Fair

Previous scholarly approaches to the Frankfurt Book Fair are a relatively select grouping: while writers' festivals have been the subject of considerable recent scholarship (for example Murray 2012; Driscoll 2014; Sapiro 2016; Weber 2018), there is less research on publishing trade fairs. One line of research is historical: Peter Weidhaas, long-time Fair director, chronicled the Buchmesse (2007, 2009). Stephan Füssel has edited two collections with a predominantly historical focus, including Ulrike Seyer's work on the Buchmesse during the 1960s (Füssel 1999; Altenhein and Füssel 2007; Seyer 2007). Sabine Niemeier's monograph takes an overview of the Fair's history to the (then) present day (2001).

Other research has been more anthropological or sociological in orientation. In this vein is work by Brian Moeran (2010, 2011), including his article 'The Book Fair As Tournament of Values' (2011), which draws on Pierre Bourdieu's model of the literary field and Arjun Appadurai's concept of 'tournaments of value'. Approaches from cultural sociology include Roanna Gonsalves' work, which adapts Bourdieusian thinking to analyse the Frankfurt Book Fair's dynamics, showing how Indian publishers (2015) mobilise friendliness as a strategy.

In publishing studies and book history the Frankfurt Book Fair has been discussed in trade-oriented books such as Lynette Owen's *Selling Rights* (eighth edition, 2019), in Corinna Norrick-Rühl's examination of the Fair in the context of the broader international book market (2019), and in publications by John B. Thompson (2010) and Simone Murray (2012), whose main interest is in the evolving role of the Fair since the 1990s as it widened its focus from books to encompass content and rights. A special issue of *Mémoires du Livres/Studies in Book Culture* includes articles on the Frankfurt Book Fair (Hertwig 2020; Norrick-Rühl 2020). These accounts are especially attuned to the role of the Buchmesse in the commerce of publishing, including its role in the creation of bestsellers.

Each of these accounts is productive and finds a place in the chapters of our book. At the same time these accounts all acknowledge their limitations, particularly in relation to the layered complexity of the Frankfurt Book Fair, limitations that have prompted us towards the creative approach of Ullapoolism outlined in the previous section.

Bestsellers

One of the challenges in researching the Frankfurt Book Fair is the high numbers of individuals and organisations that participate. The same problem of proliferation applies to the study of books at Frankfurt. As an element of the 'bestsellers' thread in the Cambridge Elements in Publishing and Book Culture series, this book takes a special interest in the interplay between the Buchmesse and bestsellers, and thereby advances existing scholarship on the topic.

One of our key research findings in this book is that the Frankfurt Book Fair is essentially forward-looking, and nowhere is its optimism more manifest than in the Buchmesse's concentration on the production of future bestsellers. Bestsellers are the high-profile products that drive publishing as an industry and connect it to other media sectors. Bestsellers are also the public face of the industry, the items which, in the words of one individual in the trade, make it '"interesting to the outside world; they are barometers of public taste, the harbingers of the new"' (Mitchinson, cited in Squires 2007, 106). For John Sutherland, examining the sociology of bestsellers is 'like running one's fingers over a topographical map of . . . social history' (Sutherland 2002, 7).

And yet, despite (or perhaps linked to) the bestseller's potency in publishing and society more generally, the term 'bestseller' has no clear, stable meaning. Industry definitions are highly constructed and contested, with books opportunistically named bestsellers on their covers long before they are published or a single copy sold. Bestseller lists, even in the age of Nielsen BookScan's rich sales data, are both 'marketing tool and historical fiction' (Miller 2000), editorialised, manipulated and missing key sales outlets (such as Amazon) and book types (including from the burgeoning world of self-publishing). The unit of time over which bestsellers are counted – an hour on Amazon, the week in a newspaper, the year in an industry round-up, the decade in a reflective commentary – slips and slides, creating an additional yet imprecise vocabulary of fast, steady and long-sellers (Escarpit 1966; Sutherland 1981).

Previous academic work has traced the historical development of the bestseller, frequently approaching it more as a genre (that is, mass market genre fiction) than a quantitative descriptor (Mott 1947; Escarpit 1966; Sutherland 1978, 1981; Bloom 2002; Gelder 2004). Over time bestsellers have become more and more important to the industry; as the success of the Harry Potter series highlights, the gulf is increasing between the highest-selling titles and the very long tail (Steiner 2014).

Our Ullapoolist conceptualisation of bestsellers incorporates each of these overlapping, fluid definitions and proposes another approach: the bestseller as situation. Bestsellers, we argue, are actively constructed situations in book culture. They are the products of people, practices, sites, materials and events, and they are the instigators of further activity: buying, reading, imitating, avoiding. Our use of the word 'situation' intentionally recalls the Situationist International's provocative activities, but whereas their situations had an overtly disruptive political purpose, the political impact of bestsellers often seems conservative, reproducing dominant neo-liberal market values. And yet, we suggest, the sheer scale, reach and variety of activity that surrounds bestsellers means they are both generative of and generated by the broader political and economic dimensions of book culture. Bestsellers are situations that both confirm and disrupt patterns of global book commerce and the scholarship that attends to it. Bestsellers are, thus, also the instigating purpose of this study, although – as detailed later – we excavate beneath them over the course of this book.

One aim of this book then is to discern the workings that produce international bestsellers before the fact: the meetings, deals and marketing efforts that take place at the global source. Bestsellers travel globally through rights deals across multiple territories and formats. Bestsellers also depend upon the generation of word-of-mouth marketing, and Frankfurt is where global buzz campaigns begin in earnest. The Fair is the omphalos of international bestsellers, and studying it sheds new light on how these important but often ill-defined products are produced and circulated.

Methods: Ullapoolism Goes to the Buchmesse

The Buchmesse is a compressed, intense layering of social, technological, cultural and commercial transactions, and its scale and organisational complexity pose a methodological challenge for book culture researchers. It has travelled through centuries and existed in its current orientation through decades, and each year it is remade through the minutiae of daily schedules, half-hourly meetings, minutes of activity, seconds of chance encounters and split-second decisions on which route to take through the Fair. The Fair is multilingual, multicultural and literally multilevel with intersecting experiences across parallel, never quite touching worlds. Activity at the Fair builds cumulatively, palimpsest-like, as the Fair expands and contracts and as old hands and new eyes bring their understandings, experiences, ennui and excitement to the event. What is needed, perhaps, is an excavation of the Frankfurt Book Fair. Beneath the surface of the industry discourse that surrounds Frankfurt is a world to explore.

What methods might researchers use to account for, travel through, situate themselves within and even recreate such a polyvalent entity as the Buchmesse? And in seeking to understand the trajectories bestselling books and their authors, publishers and readers have travelled to their eventual success, how might their stories be told? Our approach builds on the scholarship outlined earlier in this book, but furthers it via Ullapoolism's incorporation of arts-informed thinking and embodied, participatory modes.

We carried out our research for this book over three consecutive years of fieldwork at the Frankfurt Book Fair (2017–19). We conducted fifty-two interviews, walked the Buchmesse and surrounding areas of Frankfurt, sat in on dozens of meetings, and attended multiple parties and events. We also carried out a host of arts-informed research projects: we measured things, handed out fortune-telling mood fish, set up our own publisher stand in a disused area of Hall 6, took on the personae of journalists, and wrote a novella. A complete list of methods (many of which, whether traditional or creative, incorporate aspects of the dérive or the détournement) is detailed in Table 1. Our argument is that this eclectic suite of methods produces situated knowledge of the Fair and its role in the book industry; playful methods, in particular, follow the epistemology of Ullapoolism in revealing hard-to-access qualitative information about the lived experience, commercial effects and political fault lines of the Buchmesse.

Table 1 Methods used in this book, and the chapter reporting their results

Paper Planes	Introduction
Participant Observation, Including Parties	1, 2, 3
Reading (books, media articles, tweets using the official Frankfurt Book Fair hashtag)	Introduction, 1, 2, 3, Conclusion
Interviews	1, 2, Conclusion
Fortune-Telling Mood Fish	1
Industry Newsletter Collages	1
Penny Power and Polly Pringle, Journalists	1, 3, Conclusion
The Cardboard Buchmesse	2
Laser Measuring	2
The Publisher Stand Reversed	2
The Frankfurt Kabuff, a comic erotic novella by Blaire Squiscoll	2, 3
The Sleaze-O-Meter	3
Spotify Playlist	3
Custom Tote Bags	3
Non-actualised Method 1: Stickers	3
Non-actualised Method 2: Burning It Down	3
Guess Who Am I	Conclusion

We also recognise the limitations of our methods. Our participation was both enabled and constrained by our existing networks amongst anglophone publishers (particularly UK and Australian), although the book industry contacts we developed became more geographically and linguistically diverse as our networks expanded. We also recognise that the Buchmesse is not one event but many, and it is impossible to produce a full understanding of it. Without Hermione Granger's Time-Turner (borrowed from *Harry Potter and the Prisoner of Azkaban*), we were physically limited by how much we could observe. The epistemology of Ullapoolism acknowledges these constraints, but also (as future chapters articulate) actively creates its modes of understanding and interpretation through them.

This short book, then, looks at a big topic – the Frankfurter Buchmesse, the world's largest publishing industry event – and its role in circulating bestselling books. It explores the transnational flows of information in the publishing industry, the sales of rights that are so essential to bestsellers and the physical pathways that enable them. It analyses the racial and gender politics of the Fair, as well as the political turmoil that occasionally intrudes into cosmopolitan, bookish discourse.

We begin in Chapter 1 by asking, what and where is Book Buzz? We track the physical, digital and print conversations held during and beyond the Fair in order to map a pattern of the buzz production that is essential to the promotion of any bestselling title. We assess the mood of the Fair and talk to book people in their element.[3] Chapter 2 analyses the physical spaces of the Buchmesse which, we show, express power relations within the industry that affect the circulation of books and book people. We examine the stand structures: their size and spaces, their displays and strategic non-displays of power and aggression. We get behind the scenes at the Fair and into 'Kabuffs'.

Hot on the heels of our entry into the Buchmesse's cupboards and other spaces, the third element in our narrative is carnivalesque. In Chapter 3 we examine the ways in which the Fair functions outside the everyday operations of the publishing industry, even as it is integral to them. The Fair is carnivalesque and licences a range of convivial, sociable and excessive behaviours. This chapter also considers the public-facing elements of the Fair – including its cosplay areas – its politics of inclusion and exclusion, as well as the unrest that has troubled the Buchmesse.

Our thrilling conclusion begins with a sociologically inflected game that surveys the interactions of different people attending the Fair. It then summarises three key themes that traverse this book: the Frankfurt Book Fair's prevailing optimism, its neoliberal self-satisfaction and its excesses

---

[3] Technically paper is not an element, but if it were, we imagine it would be the publisher's.

(including environmental). This book demonstrates how, in order to succeed, bestsellers must travel through large, ravelled, deep-reaching networks at the Buchmesse.

***

Imagine a woman on a plane reading a book. It's a recent bestseller, a thriller, and she bought it at the airport bookshop. The colophon on the spine belongs to a New York-based multinational company, but the first publisher was a small press in Tbilisi. Distribution in India is being handled by a Delhi-based start-up. These are the paper people who go to Frankfurt: the editor, the publisher, the distributor. They shuffle through the security queue at the Buchmesse and store their supplies in a Kabuff, they dance with a diplomat at a party in Frankfurt's red light district, they fold themselves into paper planes. They trade and gossip and network and so, together, they produce a bestseller. Let's follow this paper trail.

1 Book Buzz

A fish flips in the hand of a publisher. A bee flies across the hall. Alerted by the waggle dance, more bees arrive. The journalist taps a note on her phone. Buzz.

The buzz that surrounds a bestselling title can feel organic and mysterious. All of a sudden, a book seems to be 'in the air', everywhere and nowhere. But the creation of book buzz takes concerted effort. As an essential marketing component of any bestselling title, buzz itself is a key product of the publishing industry – and the Frankfurt Book Fair is one of the chief engines of its production.

This chapter begins by theorising what buzz is and how it fits with established models of book publishing. It then presents our theory of buzz at the Buchmesse. We argue that buzz at Frankfurt exists in two main states: as market-ready reports in the mainstream media, and as soft, partial, lived experiences at the Fair. This chapter analyses each of these buzz states and their function in the contemporary publishing industry, and then investigates movement between them – how information exchanged at Frankfurt in one-on-one rights sales meetings or informally at a party might turn into a trade press report or social media post, and how industry news might shape and inform the behaviour of people at the Fair.

Alongside our investigation of buzz is one of mood, which both our interviews and – as described in more detail later – our fortune-telling fish helped us to establish. We propose a typology of mood at the Buchmesse that ranges from high excitement about individual books, to general positivity related to the forward-facing nature of the Fair and the industry, via a lower mood related to physical tiredness or following unsuccessful meetings, through to negative moods relating to remembrance of things past, mental tiredness, ennui or lack of autonomy.

Like the other chapters in this book, the methods used in this chapter arise from our three consecutive years of fieldwork at the Frankfurt Book Fair. For this chapter in particular, we gathered and read numerous industry newsletters and media articles on the Fair, as well as collecting and qualitatively analysing tweets using the official hashtag #fbm19. We also sat in on and observed dozens of one-on-one meetings and attended numerous formal and informal functions, both planned and by the mode of the dérive.

In order to explore and get beyond typical lines of industry discourse, we supplemented these methods by conducting fifty-two 'vox pop'-style (that is, very brief) interviews. In accordance with our ethics process, participants were emailed transcripts of their interview and provided consent for their use in this book. We recruited interviewees using a snowball sample that began with our UK and Australian networks and rapidly expanded to include people from India, the United States, Hong Kong, Germany, China and the Middle East. Our interviewees included people working for publishing services providers, independent contractors and Fair organisers and publishers both large and small, though leaning more towards independent publishers than multinational publishers. Our interviews were evenly split between men and women, a ratio that does not reflect the apparent gender make-up of the Fair (where women predominate, although not in the most powerful positions) but does perhaps speak to the dynamics of our interview process: men may be more inclined to talk and have more freedom in the allocation of their time.

Our interviews consisted of only two questions (plus follow-up prompts): (1) who was your last meeting with and what did you discuss, and (2) what was the mood of the meeting? In a détournement of the interview process, we concluded each interview by giving the participant a red cellophane fortune-telling fish to hold in the palm of their hand. The movement of the cellophane was decoded according to a legend: if the fish curled up, the participant was 'passionate', if it flipped over, the participant was 'silly', and so on. Other Ullapoolist methods used in this chapter include ripped paper collages détourned from print versions of industry newsletters and inhabiting the personae of the journalists Penny Powers and Polly Pringle. Together, these methods creatively explore elements of buzz, mood and their links to the international production and discussion of bestsellers, underpinning what we term 'publishing buzzness'.

Theorising Book Buzz

Buzz, as we are interested in it, operates on a number of levels: as marketing for a specific book (its most focused manifestation, and particularly relevant in the case of bestsellers); as marketing for a sector of the publishing industry, often a genre or format; and as marketing for the industry as a whole. In addition, buzz generates positive publicity for the Frankfurt Book Fair itself. Buzz therefore has a complicated typology which intersects with several other key concepts, chief among them marketing and mood.

The Buchmesse takes place in Germany, but German has no word for buzz: German publishers use the English term. This English word evokes most immediately the activity of bees – now a critically endangered species and, perhaps not coincidentally, the subject of several buzz-worthy, bestselling books in recent years (notably *The History of Bees* (2015) by Maja Lunde). Individual bees buzz as part of their general movement from A to B, but buzz is most strikingly generated as part of a swarm. Swarms happen periodically and can involve tens of thousands of bees on the move. The metaphor here for publishing is strong and can be further extended. Just as bees construct cells in a honeycomb, so individual actors at Frankfurt can be found working on spreadsheets, constructing profit and loss statements, cash flow and balance sheets cell by cell. Noise is undergirded by structure, by hard work and by productivity.

Both Moeran (2011) and Gonsalves (2015) discuss Frankfurt buzz, the latter as a kind of word-of-mouth marketing linked to informal social networks and dealmaking. For Thompson (2010) broader publishing industry buzz around 'big books' (a concept similar to the category of bestsellers) 'is a performative utterance, a type of speech act that is a pervasive feature of the field of trade publishing' (2010, 193), which he distinguishes from hype. In Thompson's formulation hype is positive talk about a book by those with an interest in selling it; buzz is created when there is an affirmative response (including financial investment) from a buyer. Thompson describes specific practices, such as auctions, as 'buzz machines' (2010, 208) generating collective belief in the potential of a book. Buzz is at the core of an industry built on future expectations and risk: 'In the absence of anything solid, nothing is more persuasive than the expressed enthusiasm (or lack of it) of trusted others' (2010, 194). Authors must convince agents, who must convince acquiring editors, who must convince their own in-house sales and marketing teams and directors that a book will be enjoyable and successful (Squires 2020), and this is done through buzz.

Buzz as a communicative act has ongoing effects outside the industry as it spills over into mainstream and social media, literary organisations, reading groups and individual readers, becoming part of the broader act of marketing books (Squires 2007). Clement, Propp and Rott (2007) usefully develop an understanding of buzz in their description of books as 'hedonic' goods which are difficult to sample. Unlike music, they argue, it is hard to get a 'taste' of a book; this makes the word of others who have read it carry more weight than for other products. This attribute is particularly the case for those outside the industry, i.e. readers. As Clement and colleagues write, because books are 'hedonic products, or products whose consumption leads to fantasies and emotional arousal', thorough assessment prior to consumption is effectively impossible; as a result, 'awareness and word-of-mouth effects seem crucial' (Clement et al. 2007, 78).

In the academic discipline of marketing, buzz is less specifically defined. It is, for example, 'contagious talk about a brand, service, product, or idea', such as teenagers 'buzzing' products to their friends or neighbours bringing chicken sausages to a backyard barbeque (Carl 2006, 602). This kind of buzz production is akin to the work of the social media influencer and is accompanied by ethical challenges that are less acute in the industry context of a publishing trade fair (although the Fair has its own informal spaces and friendship networks; Chapter 3 discusses some of the issues that attend these). It is useful to keep the broader definition of buzz as 'contagious talk' in mind, though, to see some of the layers and variety of buzz at work in the production of bestsellers at the Buchmesse.

Buzz Produced in the Mainstream Media

The first type of buzz we examine is perhaps the loudest: journalistic commentary surrounding the Frankfurt Book Fair, including most obviously those media reports that use the word 'buzz'. Say the word and buzz appears, a kind of summoning spell or self-fulfilling prophecy. This kind of buzz can be considered a hard product of the Buchmesse. Typically such buzz happens after the Buchmesse as a kind of distillation or result of the Fair's activity.

In some cases buzz happens some time after the Fair, upon a book's public release. Interest at the Buchmesse becomes part of the origin story of a book. An example of this is a review of a new thriller by Adrian McKinty which described the book as a breakout title and 'the first of [McKinty's] books to be sold at the Frankfurt Book Fair, where publishers from 24 countries snapped it up' (Steger 2019). Another example is the Australian young adult novel *Nevermoor*, 'released to a barrage of publicity . . . following an eight-publishing house international auction at the Frankfurt Book Fair. Rights have been sold into 29 territories; film rights were preempted by 20th Century Fox' (Morris 2018). These examples demonstrate how 'Frankfurt' is used to produce a kind of buzz that feeds directly into the creation of a bestseller. In other cases buzz can focus on an author. For example:

> Last week, a lavish dinner was held in [author Kate Morton's] honour at the Frankfurt Book Fair, the biggest book marketplace in the world, attended by leading publishers from around the globe. 'I don't know this has ever been done for an Australian author before,' says Robert Gorman, the chief executive of her Australian publisher, Allen & Unwin. (Williams 2012)

Morton is an unusually internationally successful Australian writer (Driscoll and Rehberg Sedo 2019), and the media claim made for her as the toast of Frankfurt reinforces her special standing as an author of global bestsellers.

Beyond these book-level and author-level accounts of buzz, media reports highlight trends shortly after the Fair and, in the process of doing so, describe book deals. Several reports in 2018 described 'up-lit' as a 'dominant trend' (Sullivan 2018) and 'the resounding trend of the fair' (Flood 2018); these articles included information about books, including Beth Morrey's *The Love Story of Missy Carmichael*, which sold for a six-figure sum after its 'publisher fought off an astonishing nine bids from rivals' (Sullivan 2018). Morrey's book was not released until February 2020, but by December 2019 it had 132 ratings and 76 reviews on Goodreads based on advanced reader copies. Media mention of Frankfurt, then, is one component of extensive pre-publication marketing.

Buzz As Lived Activity at the Frankfurt Book Fair

How do these after-the-fact media accounts of buzz relate to activity during the Fair? As we noted in the introduction, there is a gap between how the Buchmesse is reported and how it is experienced. We sought to identify the nature of this gap through our fieldwork. One of the hypotheses we considered before commencing our fieldwork was that buzz might feel more intense at the Fair, that thousands of people would be talking excitedly in the halls about the same new 'it' book or trend. This was not what we found. In our first year, 2017, we searched for the kind of book buzz familiar to us from the media and we were not able to find any. After multiple years, though, we learned where and what the buzz was at Frankfurt. We discovered that buzz, as lived activity at the Buchmesse, is dispersed and fragmented, soft and malleable, existing in the form of hints and gossip rather than public declarations. Buzz at Frankfurt is the same product as buzz about Frankfurt, but at an earlier stage of production. This is evident in some of the forms of in-Fair buzz we identified, described in what follows.

Buzz at Rights Sales Meetings

The most obvious way buzz about a potential bestseller is generated at Frankfurt is through rights meetings, where agents and publishers encourage other publishers to purchase international rights for a title: when successful, these are the deals the media report. We sat in on numerous meetings of this kind and heard of others through our interviews. When we interviewed Arpita Das, founder and publisher of Yoda Press in India, she had just had a meeting with a publisher at University of Queensland Press: 'We talked about a book of poetry by an Indian origin woman that they've published and I want to buy rights to that. And she is interested in young adult, the short fiction book that we've published.'

Our interviewee Chrysothemis Armefti of 2 Seas Agency described another example. When we asked about her most recent meeting she described pitching a French non-fiction title, *The Language of Birds*, to a Polish editor. For Armefti this book was 'our hot title during the Frankfurt Book Fair', and while the Polish editor wasn't interested in acquiring rights, Armefti had already received offers in other Frankfurt meetings. In such meetings the selling agent might explain to the potential buyer that rights have already been sold to other territories as a way to encourage further sales. As mentioned in the introduction, these rights sales meetings are frequently described as the core business of the Frankfurt Book Fair.

Temporally and in terms of format these meetings spill outside the Fair – in person in the days and nights around the Fair, or via phone, Skype and email in advance of, during and after the Fair. Several of our interviewees articulated the importance of follow-up, and it shaped their behaviour during the Fair. From a rights seller's perspective, digital communications after the Fair can be even more important than a meeting. Greg Bain from the Australian Publishers' Association told us:

> People will look at books at Frankfurt, but then when you get
> home there's hundreds and hundreds of books that they've
> expressed an interest in, and they come pouring in the door all
> at once in October, and you've got to try and find a way of
> getting above the noise with that publisher or that agent and
> it's a real challenge. So Frankfurt's really the first step.

From a buyer's perspective awareness of the volume of post-Fair work can create a need to temper enthusiasm. Hans Christian Rohr of C. Bertelsmann was mindful of creating realistic expectations: 'I should be polite on one hand and strict on the other, to say how many manuscripts can I read after the book fair when I have like 50 to 60 appointments and there are two to five books which are pushed into my direction at each meeting.'

Frankfurt thus extends beyond its temporal boundaries and deals and the buzz rights meetings they generate happen digitally as well as in person. As Matthew Kirschenbaum and Sarah Werner write, 'the media ecology in which contemporary authorship, book publishing, and reading now finds itself' is heavily digitised, and 'the barriers between the "virtual" and the material are becoming ever more permeable' (Kirschenbaum and Werner 2014, 408, 407). This is as true for the production of bestseller buzz as it is for other aspects of publishing and book culture.

While discussions about deals happen year round, many of our interviewees spoke to us about how agents can create pre-Frankfurt buzz and Frankfurt-adjacent deals by sitting on material over the European summer. The aim, they told us, is to get initial deals in the four weeks leading up to the Fair – ideally in large territories, including anglophone ones – in order to create pre-Frankfurt media reports and hence buzz. Armefti discussed how her 'hot title' had been 'pre-empted in quite a few countries in the last two weeks', for example.

Former rights seller and the current director of literature for the Australia Council of the Arts Wenona Byrne described to us a conversation in which colleagues, former VIPS (Visiting International Publishers, an Australian scheme), had told her about an agent sending out a book widely just before Frankfurt; they told Byrne that 'nobody would be making big offers on that book if it wasn't being sent out just before Frankfurt.' Byrne reflected on the massaging of Frankfurt time:

> Sometimes books are positioned. The timing of when they are sent out by agents and scouts is almost what defines how big they are, especially if it's sent out by an agent with a very big reputation for doing that. They were saying another agent had sent a book out on Friday night before Frankfurt and wanted offers really quickly. That kind of thing … pitches it at a certain level. It's like, drop everything, read this, this is going to be the book of Frankfurt … And so that's the power of the timing. It's also a bit manipulative though and I think a lot of editors don't like that feeling … it's kind of creating an anxiety in people who think that maybe they're going to miss out on something really, really big and I have heard that some people at least register interest in some books that they have no intention of buying, just so that they're kept in the loop about what's happening.

In Byrne's account the buzz-creating action – the release of information, the pressure to make an offer, the attraction or repulsion of buyers – takes place over email. Ultimately, while it might hypothetically be possible for a buyer to offer a seven-figure advance for a debut novel in a rights meeting at Frankfurt, it is far more likely that deals are done over email and decided in acquisitions meetings, negotiated with more care than a half hour slot at a busy fair allows. But the half hour meeting still has several important functions: to give a first glance at new titles, to provide further context for a title emailed as a PDF, or to shake hands symbolically and celebrate a deal concluded.

Although offers are made at the Fair, then, the Buchmesse more evidently functions as a networking site. For many meetings relationship building is more important than pitching any individual book. A meeting can be used to connect with someone of importance in the publishing ecosystem, to learn the taste of this person, and to sow the seeds for deals years ahead when the right match comes along (for more on the networked development of publishers' tastes see Squires 2017). Soft connections – enquiring about the other person's family or pets – turn into long-term relationships that build extensive and deep networks that in turn produce business deals, as Moeran also identified (2011, 90). So even for those participating in the core business of rights sales meetings, buzz as lived activity at the Fair is rarely a one-off, big deal event as portrayed in the media, but rather consists of myriad preparatory and ancillary components that may one day be shaped into a newsworthy deal. A big deal may not even be the goal – a long-term, steady, money-making relationship (involving numerous midlist authors, for example) may be much more important and valuable to all parties than a single, spectacular high-risk sale.

The relational component of dealmaking means that informal meetings are also important sites for the production of buzz at the Fair. Cordelia Borchardt from S. Fischer told us that her most recent meeting was:

> with an old friend but also publisher and we were gossiping, but in the course of gossip he was telling me about a book that he acquired which is going to be big in the United States and which might be interesting for my list as well. I would

not have heard about it in any other way because the book
fair is about talking and sometimes unexpected talking.

Another publisher from New Zealand, when we asked about his last meeting, said:

> Well, there's formal and there's informal, isn't there? So
> I had our last formal meeting at about four o'clock,
> which was a complete washout. But then I've had these
> informal meetings since where somebody just wanders
> up and has a glass of wine, and goes 'I quite like that
> book you've got.'

When we asked Canongate rights director Andrea Joyce about her last meeting she told us:

> The last meeting I had was with . . . a Finnish publisher and
> I managed brilliantly to arrive too late for the meeting
> because . . . the train wasn't working and the tram wasn't
> working either . . . on the way here I spoke to [. . .] as we
> walked in, who's a lovely German publisher and I talked to
> her about a book. And then I got here [to her stand] I called
> [the Finnish publisher] and I texted him and I emailed him
> and he came back.

Joyce's anecdote shows how, for a productive seller, rights sales conversations (here, with a German publisher) can be jammed into incidental spaces at the Fair – while walking into the Messe, on public transport or between meetings. Interactions take place across text message and email as well as in person.

Happenstance meetings in the halls and spaces of the Buchmesse can also lead to seemingly fortuitous matches between publishers and books. Australian author Heather Rose tells such a story in relation to an international rights sale for her book. She describes being:

in New York to meet my US publisher. That, in itself, is
a story of wonder. Some months before, I was introduced to
a German publisher in Sydney. I spoke to him for less than
four minutes. I learnt later that he obtained a copy and read
my novel on the plane back to Germany but was unable to
convince his publishing firm to take the novel on. At the
Frankfurt Book Fair, a month or so later, he saw
a New York colleague. He took her by the arm, walked
her to my book, put it in her hands and said, 'This is for
you.' It turned out he was right. (Rose 2018)

The apparent serendipity of this story has carefully orchestrated components,
both in the decision-making and in its recounting by the author. Similar
combinations of the calculated and the spontaneous also happen in larger
informal gatherings. Parties are ideally constructed for the circulation of buzz,
which thrives on storytelling and hooks, gossip and a sense of secrecy and inside
information (see further discussion in Chapter 3). One agent even compared the
dynamics of buzz production with a party: UK literary agent Jonny Geller
wrote of the Fair that 'having a hot book is like having a party where you have
host anxiety; not having a hot book is like going to a nice party but not being
sure why you are there and who invited you' (Geller 2018).

One of the effects of buzz produced at rights sales meetings is that it creates
a perception of a concentric circle model of buzz; some people at Frankfurt feel
closer to the centre than others. Many of the people we spoke to described their
work – or to be more precise, given our interview questions, their last meeting –
as not the 'real' Frankfurt. This might have been the result of our method,
which was designed to elicit granular information about a range of meetings,
rather than allowing participants to talk about what they deemed to be their
most meaningful or important encounter. Those whose work is back-to-back
rights sales meetings might have more confidence about their centrality and
importance, but this might be matched by exhaustion and not being able to see
beyond their own stand, or a sense of deals going on elsewhere. Almost
everyone at Frankfurt feels like they are missing something, which is connected
to the processes of inclusion and exclusion investigated further in Chapter 3.
This is perhaps a version of an industrywide feeling, since publishing industry

professionals who are not at Frankfurt also experience FOMO (fear of missing out). At Frankfurt, FOMO applies even for those who make missing out on buzz a conscious decision (or lifestyle choice): who prioritise working in their hotel rooms, seeing a few close friends or long-term business associates rather than attending a party, going to bed early. This absence of buzz is also surprisingly a feature of social media.

Buzz and Social Media

While social media is an increasingly important component of book cultures and book marketing (Kirschenbaum and Werner 2014; Murray 2018), our research suggests that book-specific buzz does not tend to circulate on social media during the Buchmesse; digital tools for sharing rights sales information, for example, are confined to the more private forms of email and text messaging during the Fair. To determine this, we collected 2,085 tweets from the hashtag #fbm19 in order to analyse a snapshot of book buzz on Twitter. Most of these were in German, meaning the set of tweets in English was of a feasible size to read and perform a descriptive analysis. Our findings concerning the anglophone tweets is that they were overwhelmingly not written by individuals or companies concerned with adult trade fiction and non-fiction. Rights deals and opportunities are not discussed on social media – rather, such information is contained in private or industry communications.

What does circulate on social media during the Book Fair? The Frankfurt Book Fair twitter hashtag was primarily used by those in smaller sectors within the publishing industry. Many tweets came from accounts whose Twitter profiles aligned them with companies working in a number of niches: digital publishing services (the most common tweeters on the hashtag), self-publishing, scholarly publishing and children's publishing. It makes sense that digital services and self-publishing (which tends to be digital-first) accounts would make use of the digital promotional opportunities available to them. Academics are heavy users of Twitter (Weber and Driscoll 2019), so it is also unsurprising to see scholarly publishers active on the platform. Children's publishing is a less obvious fit for Twitter, and perhaps is most illuminating for that reason: the significant presence of tweets from children's publishers suggests that Twitter may be a strategy for those who are or feel peripheral to the industry to raise their visibility. For example, many tweets from users in these groups simply announced their stand location or speaking slot at Frankfurt. Such tweets reproduce information already available in the official programme; tweeting is a way to try and cut through the Fair's noise and be noticed. Their friendliness thus has a slight air of desperation – 'Come and visit us!' or 'Come and see us!' – but may reach the right audience and build a network.

These promotional tweets made up the bulk of anglophone tweets we analysed. Another significant set of tweets related to the public-facing components of the Fair, and were often posted by the Buchmesse's organisers or the trade press. These tweets might include links to press releases or publications, or give information about the guest of honour activities. Finally, there was one striking set of tweets from non-publishing professionals: the cosplayers who attended the public days of the Fair and posted photos of themselves and their friends. These last two sets of tweets related to the public-oriented mode of the Buchmesse, discussed further in Chapter 3. The #fbm19 tweets, overall, suggest that social media's role in buzz production is largely limited to a contribution to the Fair's mood, rather than to its bestsellers.

Buzz As Mood

What Buchmesse-related social media communicates largely is an upbeat mood. Mood is a diffuse concept (Highmore 2013) which we argue underlies the Fair's buzz production. Creating buzz requires not only commercial activity and cultivated networks, but also enthusiasm. This is affective labour that leads directly to economic profit; as Hardt argues more generally, affective labour 'has assumed a dominant position with respect to the other forms of labour in the global capitalist economy' (Hardt 1999, 90). In both formal and informal settings, online and offline, buzz is built and communicated through the individual enthusiasm of attendees for books on their lists or for services that can bring those books into being. A buoyant mood is directly linked to the prospect of success, whether at the level of individual books, a sector of the market or the industry as a whole. It is worth investigating the moods of publishing at a conceptual level in order to

1	High key excitement
2	General positivity
3	Tired but still positive
4	Experiencing difficult moments
5	Negativity, including jaded ennui and resistance

Figure 1 A mood scale of the Frankfurt Book Fair

understand how the lived and embodied experience of publishing industry professionals at the Buchmesse goes on to produce books, including bestsellers.

At a book launch in Melbourne in 2018, an author asked us both: 'What's the mood in publishing these days?' The second question in each of our interviews at Frankfurt asked what the mood of the participant's last meeting was. This deliberately vague question prompted a range of interesting replies, as did the use of the fortune-telling fish we handed to participants after the interview. The fish subtly flagged 'mood' as a term requiring thought, while also startling and delighting our participants. The word 'passionate', we noted, often resonated with participants. In other cases, the fish simply formed a social bond between us and the participants. The fish reframed the academic interview, introducing an element of playful sociality that reflected the nature of networking at the Buchmesse.

Overall, our findings about the link between buzz and mood indicate that the moods of the Frankfurt Book Fair can be categorised according to the following scale (Figure 1).

The first mood is high excitement over individual books: the specificity of this mood links it closely to the hard buzz the media produced after the Fair. An example from our interviews was Galley Beggar's publisher Eloise Millar in 2018:

> I get very excited when I'm talking about our titles, actually,
> so it's wonderful. One of the books that we've got is a 900
> page kind of feminist great American novel and I'm so
> excited about it, but I see people, I'm, like, it's 900 pages
> and it's a single sentence and people are . . . you start to talk
> about that to corporate publishers, but they're just, like, no.

Although she didn't name it in our interview, this book turned out to be
Lucy Ellmann's *Ducks, Newburyport*, which did indeed generate much buzz
on its publication in 2019.[4] It was shortlisted for the Booker Prize and won
the Goldsmith's Prize; rights have been sold into multiple territories, and
overall the title is selling very well for such an experimental literary title.
Millar's account demonstrates the delicacy required to communicate enthusiasm for this particular title, whose length and experimentation deterred
some buyers but attracted others.

Other specific-book enthusiasts we talked to included an experienced
individual returning to literary agency after working in consulting for many
years. She spoke passionately to us about a series for adults with low literacy.
Such high-key excitement is a field-specific mood; the most attractive mood of
the Fair. It requires high commitment and is undoubtedly taxing in terms of
energy levels. This mood can also appear as overly pushy. Negotiating
a balance between expressing belief in a book or author and expressing belief
in their sales potential requires some finesse, especially in sectors of the industry
such as trade publishing where art and commerce jostle.

High-key, book-specific excitement presents quite differently when it is
deployed at the level of a publisher and is more obviously a form of marketing.
One interviewee told us that their stand featured someone dressed up as
a bacteria in order to promote a title, running around and lightening the
mood of meetings. A strange version of this positive mood was on display at

---

[4] Appropriately enough one of the passages of *Ducks, Newburyport* riffs on marketing, bees and the letter Z, zooming through the marketing acronym AIDA
(Awareness-Interest-Desire-Action) and 'buzzworthy' products, adding 'the fact
that Z is the best letter in the alphabet, because it comes at the end, and it's jazzy
and buzzing and fizzy, the fact that zebras starts with Z' (Ellmann 2019, 357, 358).

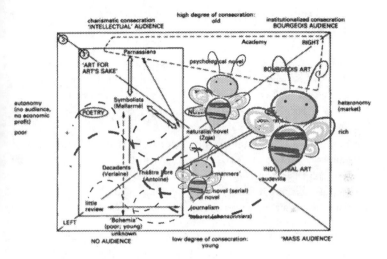

Figure 2 The field of buzz production

the Amazon stand in the German-language hall, discussed further in Chapters 2 and 3. In 2019 the mood of Amazon's stand was buoyed by the provision of expensive canapés and drinks at the launch of the 'Amazon Crossing' logo. The women presenting at the launch discussed some of the translated titles in their programme. They were evidently passionate about these books, while also reproducing chat-bot-like corporate messaging that drew on the sociopolitical ideals of the book industry, even as Amazon's pay for translators remains a topic of controversy (Flood 2015). A third example of stand-based, high-key, book-specific mood is that deployed throughout the Literary Agents and Scouts Centre (or LitAg) in its various locations. This is a kind of anti-mood as the LitAg is deliberately plain and unadorned (as discussed further in Chapter 2), but perhaps because of this, the mood there is the highest pitched. We saw the stand where the deals for E. L. James' global megaseller, *Fifty Shades of Grey*, were made: the plainest parts of the Fair are where the most mythologised things happen. Just as Bourdieu wrote about the economic world reversed, the LitAg is perhaps buzz reversed and therefore intensified (see Figure 2).

A second and very common mood is general positivity, including such articulations of the mood of a meeting by interviewees as 'quite positive', 'cautiously positive', 'very positive', 'very friendly and chatty', 'convivial and collegial', 'uplifting', 'lovely' and 'enthusiastic'. The prevalence of such comments is key evidence for our argument that the Fair is optimistic. Logically, participants have to be broadly positive in order to function at this kind of business event; as all conversation is geared around the future, it is important to imagine success.

A third mood, and the first negative one in our typology, is lower mood due to physical circumstances, principally exhaustion from the pace of the Fair. The spirit is willing but the demands of the Fair take a toll. As Gao Hui, a rights seller for a Chinese publisher, explained, 'Everyone is a little bit exhausted, but we're still very excited to know each other's works, titles, and to talk about new books, because Frankfurt is the most fruitful book fair of the year. We're still very excited.'

Attunement to the days of the week and the times of day, and awareness of how this affects the mood of individual meetings, was evident in many of our conversations about the Fair. A German publisher told us the mood of her meeting on Friday was 'relaxed' compared to if it were on a Saturday, when it would be busier. A small publisher who had just met with the CEO of a multinational publishing company told us, 'Oh, I think because we're in day one of the Fair today, as we speak, it was very good, very buoyant, very excited. Had I had the meeting perhaps at the end of Frankfurt it might have been different but no it was very, very optimistic.' When we asked an editor at Hachette to describe the mood of her most recent meeting she said, 'Yes, really good. I think a little tired, which often happens on a Friday morning after a busy fair, but also really positive.' This kind of insight demonstrates the benefit of our-in-the-moment method: a week later this participant may well have described this only as a positive meeting, losing the granularity and nuance of the embodied toll extracted by generating buzz.

A fourth mood at the Fair is a low mood due to difficult meetings. Borchardt told us that while her recent meeting was 'very positive',

> You can have conversations which are terrifying and you
> have to be at your utmost best, when you're negotiating for

example, or when you have an agent who is not happy with what you've done for a book. And then you have to muster up all your professional knowledge and ability to stand out and say what your side of things is.

One otherwise upbeat interviewee described a challenging meeting with an agent:

She wasn't necessarily drawing me out like some agents do, so, you know, you're kind of left to pitch for yourself, and she was very difficult to read, so maybe that's one of the things that throws you as well . . . It was very difficult; she had a real New York poker face [laughing].

The low mood here relates both to the agent – who did not participate in a discourse of buzzy enthusiasm – and the seller. Another interviewee described a mood as positive despite the business challenges both participants were facing: 'The mood was actually very good. It was, well, in fact, actually what I should say is, it was good, but what we've both discussed was how hard it is.'

Finally, more serious negative moods can inhibit the production of buzz. Some long-time attendees at the Buchmesse exhibit a low mood due to jadedness. There are times when books seem to be forgotten and people forget the purpose of their attendance. Other individuals expressed nostalgia for Fairs of the past. This happened even across the three years of our fieldwork, with some publishers in 2019 expressing to us regret for things that had changed since 2017, principally the moving of the LitAg Hall from Hall 6.3 to the Festhalle (Snaije 2019), which we discuss further in Chapter 2. This was a negative mood in that it focused on changes perceived as for the worse, but it derives from a sort of cultural security (no doubt mildly enjoyable to experience) born from long-standing attendance. A different kind of negative mood may be experienced by attendees who have been compelled to come either to the Fair or to a specific event such as an after-hours party. This negative mood is caused by a lack of autonomy and agency (Chapter 3 explores further challenges around parties and power). In other cases people are compelled to represent books they don't especially like, negating the strongest buzz-producing mood of the Fair.

Converting Buzz

The preceding two sections indicate that buzz as experienced at the Fair differs markedly from buzz as reported in the media. How then does one form turn into the other? How are the lived moods of the Fair told and retold to become an aggregated 'mood' distilled into deals and trends?

One of the chief mechanisms is the trade publications, whose journalists circulate the Buchmesse and which release and distribute daily editions during the Fair. We heard rumours of these publications holding on to press releases so they have exciting content for Fair week, collapsing the temporality of the industry in order to put more focus on the Buchmesse and to increase its buzz-producing capacity. These publications also combine reports on social and informal interactions (and, in the case of *The Bookseller*, a gossip column, as discussed further in Chapter 3) with trade news. *Publishers Weekly* also includes a 'Frankfurt Briefcase' section which tips publishers off about books available for purchase.

These publications reflect the trade back to itself, winnowing millions of interactions into a smaller number of significant ones. The trade press produces summaries of the Fair that attempt to pin down its mood, as this quartet of quotes from one article demonstrates:

> 'It feels a very buzzy and buoyant fair.' – Rebecca Wearmouth, international rights director at Peters Fraser + Dunlop
>
> 'It's been a very busy fair – the atmosphere on the PRH stand is incredibly upbeat.' – Amelia Evans, rights director at Cornerstone
>
> 'It's been a hugely positive fair ... I can't remember attending a more optimistic fair.' – David Headley, D H H Literary Agency m.d
>
> 'It's been an incredibly buzzing fair.' – Karen Sullivan, publisher at Orenda Books (all quoted in Mansfield 2019)

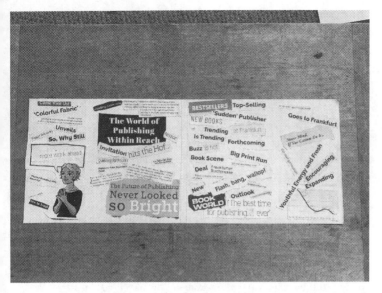

Figure 3 Collage made from industry newsletters at the 2019 Frankfurt Book Fair

Here *The Bookseller* transforms individual experiences into an upbeat narrative of the Fair and by extension the book industry. The same article discusses trends: well-being and personal development, up-lit, climate titles and biographies. It is the industry interpreting itself for itself and it paves the way for broader journalistic accounts.

As one of our Ullapoolistic methods, we created scrapbook-like collages snipped and détourned from the pages of the industry dailies, noting repeated words ('buzz', 'trending', 'hot') as well as more surprising phrases ('Flash, bang, wallop!') (see Figure 3).[5] The vocabulary and layout of these

---

[5] Note this collage is available as a printable download from the Cambridge University Press website www.cambridge.org/driscoll, formatted for use as an alternative dust jacket for this book.

industry newsletters are crucial to the distillation and communication of buzz at the Fair. This messaging is then focused even further by reports in the mainstream media about the Fair and upon the release of high-profile books.

A transition to hard buzz is also effected through press releases, particularly those produced by the Frankfurter Buchmesse itself. We saw this in action during our time as journalists Penny Powers and Polly Pringle. Using these alter egos, we attended the official opening press conference of the 2019 Buchmesse.[6] The speeches we heard held forth on the health of the book industry, the rise in audiobook sales and the growing role of AI: all key messages in describing the shape of book culture and its areas of future profit-making. In Germany, too, there are additional routes for information from the Fair to reach the public, including radio programmes, public attendance and associated events. Such mechanisms contribute to the general buzzness surrounding the Buchmesse and the industry, though not so much to buzz around individual titles.

What is lost and gained through this process? Big trends have a tendency to lose meaning through generality (what is up-lit, really?) and can often operate behind the zeitgeist (the identification of climate change books as a trend at Frankfurt 2019, for example). Smaller feelings, books and moments that might otherwise be key to industry or political change can be lost in the transition from soft to hard buzz. The Buchmesse also produces more buzz than can be converted into global bestsellers or prestige-winning books; not every buzzy book becomes a bestseller, and participants' positive mood at one Fair can be depleted only to be replaced by the messaging of the following year. The Buchmesse and the industry therefore operate through an excess of buzz and require loss as well as success to generate its forward momentum.

Conclusion: Generating Buzz at the Buchmesse

The Frankfurt Book Fair is a clearing house for transnational flows of information about books that are going to make it globally: information

---

[6] Penny and Polly also attended the arrival of Norway's Literature Train at the Hauptbanhopf, complete with brass band and crown princess, and participated in a press tour of Norway's guest of honour pavilion, witnessing the performative aspects of the guest of honour scheme.

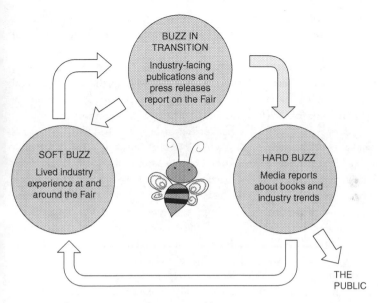

Figure 4 The communications circuit of buzz

exchanged in one-on-one meetings, on email (but not Twitter), via book auctions and in the paper newsletters handed out at the entrance to each hall in the Buchmesse. The Fair is also a marketing device in its own right, a lever for the media, publishers and authors to push as they try to create a bestseller. Exactly how this buzzness happens has been the focus of our investigation in this chapter.

This chapter's aim was to trace how buzz is produced at the Buchmesse, based on an understanding of buzz as a form of marketing essential to the creation of a bestselling book. Our argument in this chapter has been that the production of buzz involves three key stages, outlined in Figure 4.

First a kind of 'soft' buzz is produced in a dispersed and fragmented way across the online and physical spaces of the Buchmesse. This soft buzz exists as enthusiasm for books, the publishing industry and the Fair itself and is circulated through formal meetings, informal gatherings and digital communications, all of which may occur during, before and after the Fair. It exists as insider knowledge, reinforced by the way key information is not circulated via social media. Soft buzz is also modulated by the moods of the Fair, which our research reveals exist along a typology from high-key, book-specific excitement, through to general positivity, through to physical exhaustion, through to a series of downbeat moods (some of which negate buzz and some of which contribute to it through a counter-narrative).

The second stage in the production of buzz is when the soft buzz is captured and focused in industry news publications – the trade magazines that circulate during and after the Fair. This self-reflective, industry-level buzz then percolates out to become 'hard' buzz in the broader cultural media, spread through book reviews and think pieces to become the received wisdom about the industry's key titles for the year ahead: the concentration of attention that feeds into the 'winner takes almost all' model of contemporary publishing. Buzz in journalism is concretised, hard, available for use as marketing (for industry, individual publishers or books), providing aggregated and overview perspectives such as data and trends. This hard buzz then feeds into next year's meetings as industry lore ('short story collections don't sell'; 'climate change books are hot'): buzz pieces can be self-fulfilling prophecies as well as producing industry excess.

Following this examination of publishing buzzness the subsequent chapters unfold buzz further by examining first the role of the Fair's physical spaces in affecting the circulation of people and buzz, and second the disruptive social possibilities that play into and sometimes against official narratives of the Buchmesse and its commercial role.

2 Big, Small, Nowhere at All

If you tell a publishing industry insider that you are going to the Frankfurt Book Fair for the first time, they will probably advise you to wear comfortable shoes. Indeed, a Google search for 'Frankfurt book fair comfortable shoes' yields more than 3.3 million hits (for the top hits see Figure 5).

Reinforcing this message, in a more open Google search for 'Frankfurt book fair advice', three of the top four results include the tip to wear comfortable shoes: 'Wear comfortable shoes = the fair is massive' (also a top hit in the first search), 'bring spare flats if you intend to wear heels (I'm going to adhere to the publishing stereotype here and assume most rights people reading this are women)'; 'definitely pack comfortable shoes!' (Coen 2017; Garry 2017; Mautref 2018). This advice, though no doubt kindly meant, raises a host of questions. Is it as universally applicable as its frequency suggests? Is this advice, and/or the footwear industry, possibly gendered and ableist? Do some people (first-timers?) at the Buchmesse

The Insider Guide to Frankfurt Book Fair 2019 - Vol. 2 - Kitaboo
https://kitaboo.com › insider-guide-to-frankfurt-book-fair-2019-vol-2 ▾
Aug 1, 2019 - Here's an insider's guide to the Frankfurt Book Fair. ... So, it's advisable to wear comfortable footwear to avoid sore foot at the end of the day.

Frankfurt Book Fair: The Olympics of Publishing - Book ...
https://bisg.org › news › Frankfurt-Book-Fair-The-Olympics-of-Publishing ▾
Nov 1, 2019 - Everyone I spoke to had some advice: wear comfortable shoes, drink Emergen-C and try not to get sick, take every opportunity to sit down, it's a ...

11 Tips for the 2018 Frankfurt Book Fair
https://blog.gutenberg-technology.com › 10-tips-2018-frankfurt-book-fair ▾
Sep 19, 2018 - Frankfurt Book Fair, Oct 10 - Oct 14, 2018. Wear comfortable shoes = the fair is massive. Study the map of the fair - make a plan based on the ...

My Frankfurt Book Fair with... Lucy Luck | The Bookseller
https://www.thebookseller.com › insight › my-fbf-lucy-luck-871946 ▾
Oct 11, 2018 - My Frankfurt Book Fair with... ... I would advise first-timers to take comfortable shoes, enjoy meeting new people and keep slots free to walk the ...

Figure 5 Top results of a Google search for 'Frankfurt book fair comfortable shoes' (3 December 2019)

walk (or stand) more than others? How do shoes, walking and standing intersect with power relations at the Fair?

The advice about shoes hints at the embodied aspects of the Frankfurter Buchmesse, including the links between buzz, mood and exhaustion. Yet it is not only people who must navigate the physical spaces of the Fair. Intellectual property rights, information about trends, titles and services, perceptions of the health of the industry and its players: all this also flows via the Fair's physical layout. Bestselling, big books (a metaphor, though sometimes also literally true according to our measuring practices) are promoted on huge posters at the stands of big publishers (whose big stands are also partly metaphorical, as we explain later).[7] But bestsellers may travel in less obvious ways too, rolling through hallways, spending time in smaller, off-the-shelf stands, being discussed in coffee stands and on stages. In this chapter we present a strand of our fieldwork focused on how movement of people and content is shaped by the Fair's physical spaces, their functions and performativity. The much-vaunted size of the Buchmesse, we argue, can be broken down and analysed in productive ways that reveal its underlying power relations.

Our Ullapoolist sensing-thinking-doing approach, as unfolded in the introduction, was deployed in the fieldwork for this chapter. In particular we align Ullapoolism with the dérives and détournements of the Situationist International and the 'low theory' of Stuart Hall, as developed by Jack Halberstam (2011).

The specific methods that we used for this chapter include a particular form of participant observation linked to Hall's argument that theory is not an end unto itself but a detour en route to somewhere else. This conceptualisation, as Halberstam articulates, is reminiscent of the situationist mode of the dérive – a purposeful wander through physical locations, attuned to the emotions triggered by space and place, and today academically codified in psychogeography. Our observations in this chapter arise from the dérives and detours we

---

[7] For an example of these practices see https://twitter.com/Beth_driscoll/status/1130724667289849857 (Twitter post, with text that reads 'in-depth literary analysis'. The picture is a close-up of a ruler next to Haruki Murakami's novel *Killing Commendatore*. The novel's depth is five centimetres.)

practised during our time at Frankfurt, including, for example, getting lost in stairwells, going up and down on escalators and navigating through halls by random choice. As Halberstam writes, low theory is 'theoretical knowledge that works on many levels at once, as precisely one of those modes of transmission that revels in the detours, twists, and turns through knowing and confusion, and that seeks not to explain but to involve' (Halberstam 2011, 15). As we dérived, our knowledge of the Buchmesse deepened in surprising ways: from learning about the use of cupboards to metaphorically experiencing a human ricochet between stands as akin to the inside of a pinball game.

We also created a series of détournements. These included the construction of a model of the Buchmesse out of cardboard, with which we invited people to interact and reflect. We also built our own Publisher's Stand Reversed in a disused corner of a hall and acquired a laser measurer which we brought to the Fair in order to explore the significance of stand size. We augment these methods by drawing on the same set of interviews used in Chapter 1.

This chapter presents the results of these methods in two sections. The first is interested in physical structures as communicative devices between attendees and in particular how they constitute displays of power and aggression. Communication can occur through strategic use of the position of a publisher's stand, as well as its size, shape, colour and design. These displays have consequences not only on behaviours, but also upon the environment, prompting reflection on the sustainability of the Fair. Beyond the role of individual displays we consider the power relations revealed by how the organising body of the Frankfurt Book Fair allocates the Buchmesse's space. We consider moving: the controversial relocation of the LitAg and the resiting of one of the international halls. These observations culminate in our modelling of the Cardboard Buchmesse as a tool for collaborative and distributed thinking about space at the Fair.

In the second section we look at some of the less visibly performative aspects of the physical space of the Fair. In contrast to showy stands, we consider the role of non-displays: organisations without stands, which can be due to lack of funding or to strategy. We reflect on the creation of our own Publisher's Stand Reversed (the term is a play on Bourdieu's 'economic world reversed') in a disused corner of the Fair strewn with discarded furniture and rubbish. We also consider individual stands and their closed-off and hidden spaces such as cupboards. At the level of the Fair as a whole, we investigate informal meeting spaces, as well as the interstitial zones between the meetings that are the ostensible purpose of the Fair. We also explore the shrinking of the Fair as a whole: if the Buchmesse is smaller than it used to be, how is this manifested and experienced?

The two sections of this chapter, then, show how the physical structures, reversals and absences of the Fair shape and direct its activities, creating opportunities for bestsellers to circulate via the personnel and objects of the Fair, as well as creating backchannels where buzz develops. These physical spaces reinforce the disparate power of organisations and actors within the book industry at the same time as they enable the formal and informal pathways through which books (including bestsellers) are marketed from business to business.

Displays of Power and Aggression: Observations of Stands at the Buchmesse

Some of the Fair's most striking contrasts are illustrated through the arrangement of its stands. The position of publisher stands is an important way in which companies communicate their position in the industry, that is their relative status in terms of both prestige and economic power. Moeran notes the importance of this in his article on the London and Frankfurt Book Fairs; publishers often seek the same position every year (to foster a sense of stability) and may engage in years-long campaigns to shift up towards the most desirable positions on highly visible corners and aisle ends. As Moeran writes, 'Where an exhibitor has its stand and how big or small that stand is have enormous implications for its visibility in the publishing world. In this respect, book fairs function like "graphs", in that they chart the relative positions of publishers and other participants in abstract space' (2010, 146). The selection and negotiation of a stand position with the Fair organisers is also a way to communicate alliances (including co-ownership of imprints or partnerships).

In her article exploring the strategies of Indian publishers at Frankfurt Gonsalves (2015) situates her primary research within core-periphery conceptualisations of global book markets (Sapiro 2010), to which should be added Casanova's (2004) explorations of the centre and peripheries of the 'world republic of letters'. As Gonsalves explains, the 'centre' of the Buchmesse is 'understandably the German publishing industry, given that the fair takes place in that country', but she describes English-language trade publishing as 'territorially hierarchised', with UK and US conglomerates 'positioned as the establishment, and others such as Indian publishers positioned on the periphery as outsiders and newcomers' (427). The Indian publishers working for conglomerates that Gonsalves interviewed were located on parent company stands and therefore had the advantages of their prime space positioning. For smaller, independent publishers, however, their status was materialised as an estrangement from the central anglophone business via the allocation of 'peripheral space' (427).

Our fieldwork observations confirmed the enduring importance of publisher stand position. In the English-speaking international hall we immediately noticed the stands that took up immense space, from Penguin Random House's almost aisle-length stand, to the similarly large HarperCollins, and to the colloquially named 'Fortress Hachette' (a nickname that recognises its size as well as the impermeable crenellated panels of its custom stand design). It is often already published and forthcoming bestselling authors and titles that are promoted in the eye-catching displays that decorate such stands, visually linking big books to big publishers. The use of scale here – big stands, big posters, big books, big fonts for the names of bestselling authors on book cover designs – is part of a logic that travels out from the Fair into book culture. When we commented upon the size of Fortress Hachette to a friend who works for a mid-sized publisher, they replied, 'but Hachette is big', demonstrating the conflation of physical presence at the Fair and market dominance. We noticed publisher services company Nielsen BookScan in a prominent end-of-aisle position. We saw that some small publishers, such as those in 'Australia Alley', were less centrally located; others, as discussed later in the section on gaps and absences, had no stand and therefore staked no physical position at all.

In our vox pop interviews (for a description of method, see Chapter 1) several participants had just been in meetings to discuss stand positions for future years. Claudia Kaiser, Vice President Business Development of the

Frankfurt Book Fair, had just met with the Malaysian Book Publishing Association to discuss 'space for next year' (the mood of the meeting was 'Positive. Dynamic'). In our meeting with staff at another national stand they told us that they had gradually been moving their stand position over the years towards a more prominent position, interconnected with their future role as a guest of honour exhibitor.

A second element of position as a communicative device at the Buchmesse is the position of the different halls. During our fieldwork in 2019 Hall 6 hosted English-language 'International Publishers', largely from OECD countries; Hall 5 hosted 'International Publishers' from a range of regions, including Europe and Africa; Hall 4 hosted a range of book-related organisations as well as the Business Club – an area of the Buchmesse organisers promoted as an exclusive meeting hub, as discussed later. Hall 3 hosted German publishers, the LitAg was in the Festhalle, and the guest of honour pavilion was in the forum. All these halls are arranged around a central outdoor space, the agora, which also features small stands and pavilions for food and events.

Controversially, the LitAg, which takes up an entire floor of a hall, was moved from the top floor of Hall 6 by the Buchmesse organising body in 2019. This move was explained to participants as due to ongoing renovations of the Messe complex, as well as in response to the increasing need for space as more agents booked tables in the LitAg ('in 2018 the LitAg sold 538 tables, up from some 500 in 2017' (Nawotka 2019a)). The LitAg, as Chapter 1 discussed, is a dramatic space at Frankfurt where some of the most significant deals happen and future bestseller buzz is generated. Based on her Frankfurt fieldwork in 2009, Murray (2012) argues that the power and growing size of the LitAg since its 1978 inception is evidence of agents' growing centrality to the industry. Entrance is by appointment or pass only so that there is less chance of disruption by the public, authors or other trade personnel wandering past.[8] In other words, there is actual gatekeeping. The 2019 move to Festhalle was controversial because it took the agents further

---

[8]   For a satirical take on the dynamics of sneaking into the literary agents' centre, albeit the one at London not Frankfurt Book Fair, see Paul Ewen's 2014 novel *Francis Plug: How to Be a Public Author* (Norwich: Galley Beggar Press).

away from the most powerful anglophone publishers (requiring even more comfortable shoes to travel longer distances), and a petition was circulated by agents – to no avail (Tivnan 2018).

A cosplay area (discussed further in Chapter 3) was introduced to the Buchmesse in 2002 and has been extended in subsequent years. As the Fair announced in 2019, cosplay 'is moving into the traditional book fair space' from its more peripheral initial positioning, and is now spread throughout the Fair: in Halls 3 and 4, the agora, and the guest of honour forum, hewing close to 'the right neighbourhood, such as near the Asian publishers' (Frankfurter Buchmesse 2019c). The announcement of the closure of Hall 5 for renovation means the shift of its occupants into Hall 4 in 2020, with the impact, it is presumed, of ousting some of its traditional occupants such as book dealers (Nawotka 2019a). Such positional shifts re-establish the dynamics of the Fair, making some organisations and people more visible and more central than others.

Finally, in terms of position, the location of the whole Fair on the Messe site (which is also used for other trade fairs and conventions) is of significance. Frankfurt might seem to the uninitiated an odd choice of city for the world's largest book fair. But as Chapter 3 explains, there is a story here which develops from larger global and geopolitical histories. We note that Frankfurt's geographical location in Europe is a lot more convenient for some publishers than others, reflecting the hierarchical mapping of Casanova's *The World Republic of Letters* (2004), which is also further discussed in Chapter 3.

In addition to the position of the Fair itself in Frankfurt, its halls and stands, the constitutive material elements of the latter are communicative devices that affect the flow of titles. Large, impenetrable panels, small and plain off-the-shelf furniture, quirky fit-outs, hand-lettered signage, celebrity cut-outs, reception desks and other physical markers offer materialised representations of the economic and symbolic relations between multinational, mid-sized and small publishers. The pricing for different stand furniture offered by the Buchmesse (such as corner stand fit-outs) reflects differential economic capacity, alongside the increasing trend towards exhibitors designing their own stands and thereby demonstrating their habitus. Moeran reflects that this is 'a kind of conspicuous consumption, as large, wealthy publishers splash out tens of thousands of pounds on stands'. Bespoke designs allow exhibitors to 'establish a form of "brand identity"' which they can transport to other international fairs' (Moeran 2010, 147). Lise Skov (2006, cited by Moeran 2010) argues that '"the condition of comparability"' at a trade fair allows exhibitors to:

> appear free of history, geography and social context; all traces of production are removed from the samples. What is visible at its booth in the fair is only the company's current market position in relation to other companies. Insofar as a company has a reputation, that reputation has to be re-enacted by aid of modular props. (Moeran 2010, 767)

We saw examples of this during our dérives. The white, brickwork-like panels of the enormous Fortress Hachette, for example, were in 2017 and 2018 arranged around a central 'panopticon' tower (or 'Crow's Nest', as its staff call it) – an elevated circular meeting space reached by a spiral flight of stairs. In 2018 we were invited up to the panopticon, from which we looked down upon other publisher stands, revelling in an impression of power and superiority. We were told this is where the 'big dogs' meet, and indeed only blue-suited men were in the panopticon when we visited. As mentioned earlier, Hachette's physical manifestation at the Fair blends seamlessly into an impression of its market dominance. But by 2019 the panopticon was gone – one informant told us that the reason for this was to provide more space as the company expanded and acquired smaller companies.

For many publishers, a low-key, off-the-shelf stand is a function of their small size and limited budget (see DW 2006). Other small publishers shared collective stands, such as that hosted by Publishing Scotland, sacrificing some of their individual branding as a result. Stand size is important to exhibitors: one stand holder told us their stand was seventy-two square metres and, whipping out our laser measurer, we replied, 'We'll be the judge of that.' (As it transpired, our measurer proved both difficult to operate and comically imprecise, but it nonetheless prompted some interesting conversations.) Another exhibitor encouraged us with a wave of his arm to admire the size of his stand, a metonymic expression of his business' buoyancy.

Material messaging in stand design extends beyond the economic into the symbolic, then, but also to considerations of comfort, national and regional cultures, design aesthetics and intended audiences. Staff at one collective national stand told us proudly of the anti-fatigue floor they had installed in order to help those tired feet and emphasised its wood panelling. They were keen to avoid stereotypical, clichéd signifiers of their country, although the dominant colour was the same as the national flag. Over in the German hall, the stands were very beautiful, and many had bars or cafés in the middle – perhaps reflecting their dual audience of the trade and, at the weekend, the German public.

Amazon offered an intriguing example of the manipulation of visual messaging through stand design. Despite Amazon's powerful role in the book industry, it had no stand replicating its scale. In 2017 we were struck by its position tucked into a corner of the German-language hall and representing its publishing and self-publishing operations, rather than its retail platform. Its decor was subdued and non-intrusive. By 2018 and 2019 Amazon had moved into a more prominent central position, albeit still in the German hall. Its stand design of wooden tree cut-outs communicated, to us, friendly mid-size publisher. Amazon's presence at the Fair is growing but remains at odds with its predatory reputation, dominance over online selling and the e-book market, and the warehouse it operates at Koblenz, an hour or so drive from Frankfurt. Amazon uses the Frankfurt Book Fair for purposes that suit its own particular agenda, such as recruiting German self-publishers or promoting its translation programme. The size and presentation of Amazon's stands at Frankfurt do not demonstrate Amazon slowly catching up to large publishers, but rather show its indifference to traditional modes of displaying status and its reconfiguration of power in the book industry.

A different kind of messaging happens at the powerful LitAg. As we discussed in Chapter 1, the room is precisely marked out and seemingly devoid of signifiers. In this hall uniformity reigns. Every stall looks exactly the same – a conspicuous and indeed dramatic design denial which belies the agents' powerful presence. Meanwhile, in the agora, size, shape and design are used to communicate a festive atmosphere. Signing boxes for authors are small plywood constructions, making the authors seem like little puppets in a theatre or actors on television, while food and beverage outlets are designed in the shape of a giant iced tea bottle or a gaily painted red caravan.

Design, positioning and size all contribute, then, to the messaging of individual stands, the halls and the Buchmesse as a whole, as well as to the economic and symbolic forces present at the Fair. The fabrication of the Buchmesse, though, presents further issues to consider. One of the consequences of using both size and custom fit-outs to communicate market positioning is the level of waste thereby generated and its consequences for environmental sustainability. We were told of stand fitters ripping out carpet and throwing it away after the event along with thousands of unused catalogues, book proofs and cardboard boxes, further evidenced in photographs in online reports (for example, Hessenchau 2019). The annual construction of this, the world's biggest book fair, is also at its end an act of destruction and waste. These physical aspects of the Buchmesse link to its annual excess of buzz, discussed in Chapter 1.

Experiment: The Cardboard Buchmesse

Materiality makes us think and, as Ullapoolists, we used materiality to extend the observations gleaned from our dérives into a détournement of the Fair itself. In 2018 a Creative Scotland spokesperson reflected on Frankfurt's capacity to enable meetings between people from around the globe. 'Frankfurt offers the world in miniature,' she wrote, in its co-location of publishers from across the world (Creative Scotland 2018). But does it? Could we see the shape of the global publishing industry mapped across the Buchmesse's multiple halls? And what would a miniaturised Frankfurt look like? To find out, and to extend our ideas about physical actions and reactions at the Fair, we created the Cardboard Buchmesse.

The aim of our experiment was to use the process of making (and playing with) a miniature, cardboard book fair to reflect upon physical elements and experiences at Frankfurt. Our equipment included cardboard, rulers, Stanley knives, scissors, glue, rubber bands and assorted found items. Using photographs and our memories of the Buchmesse in 2017 to

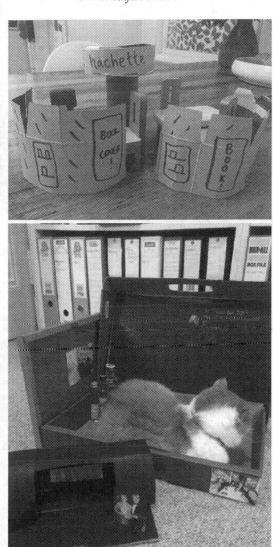

Figure 6 Prototypes of our Buchmesse model

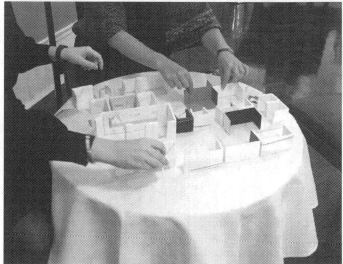

Figure 7 The Cardboard Buchmesse in action

guide us, we initially made prototypes of different elements of the Fair, including a doll's house-sized version of the Hachette stand (including its panopticon), and a cat-sized version of the Business Club (Figure 6).

Extending these ideas, we began the task of modelling an entire hall. Our first stand was a generic shell as advertised online by the Buchmesse. We then made bespoke variations, using a range of coloured and textured cardboards to create stands of different sizes (see Figure 7). We chose not to particularise via words or images in this modelling, in order to focus upon the materials and dimensions of the stands as communicative devices, as we had observed during our dérives around the Buchmesse.

Our reflections while making the Cardboard Buchmesse included scale; we made one deliberately overlarge stand to gesture at the unequal sizes we had observed. Discussions during our construction phase included the observation that large stands of multinational publishers were 'both closed and open, emotionally speaking', and one of us wondered whether we should make them 'castellated, with potential for boiling oil to be poured from the ramparts'. The experimentation with custom designs and unique fit-outs was sometimes frustrating – at one point one of us threw a model stand into the air – but also produced intriguing objects.

We trialled placing the stands in different configurations in order to explore relations between them. Then we took it on the road (in a cardboard box), inviting friends and colleagues – most of whom had not been to Frankfurt – to interact with the Cardboard Buchmesse. With them, we arranged and rearranged the stands, commented upon the dynamics of different physical layouts, and imagined ways in which people might move between stands: via a slingshot, becoming stuck, desperately searching for an exit.

When one colleague was a little unsure how to begin arranging the stands, we prompted them by asking, 'What would Pascale Casanova say?' Unprompted, participants frequently gave voice-overs for their arrangements. This narrativisation was encouraged by the absence of printed words and images on the model, which gave people creative freedom. Our colleagues reflected on the attributes of and differences between the stands. These reflections were mostly to do with size, but sometimes also focused on the materials used: one participant wondered which were the fixed or permanent-seeming features of stands, which were more flimsy or less substantial, and how this might relate to the status of the publishers. Statements made about the stands included: 'This is a new children's publisher; they spent quite a lot of money on their stand; they've got a cutesy but subtle vibe going on,' and 'Here's a laneway; there's going to be some faux graffiti put in there.' Someone noted of one stand, 'these people are quite brash,' but another was 'solid as a rock'.

Overall, three key patterns emerged through playing with and reflecting on the Cardboard Buchmesse. First, grouping by size was a recurrent activity. One person put all the small stands together, thinking that orga- nisers would have 'relegated' them to a back corner, but that this might come with advantages: communality, shared social spaces and some peace and quiet. This person also grouped all the larger stands, thinking they would have their own exclusive area. This didn't quite tally with our observations of the actual Buchmesse, which to some extent mixes large, mid-sized and small, meaning that each multinational dominates its own aisle. One participant, while initially 'not sure what signifies what', also wanted to group by size, saying, 'I imagine the big things are at the centre with the smaller things orbiting them.'

This behaviour, we suggest, shows a recognition, or even a tendency to reinforce, the affinities and power structures that exist in the publishing industry and in book culture more generally. Book culture tends to be marked by at least superficial 'niceness' and conviviality, a searching for commonality and similarities, for like-mindedness and affiliation, that can be both productive in terms of cooperation and a way to obscure or make bearable the underlying patterns of neoliberal conglomerate power.

Second, the unusual-looking stands in our model – the outliers – prompted considerable discussion. Our one oversized stand had been designed to represent a multinational, conglomerate publisher. The power- ful pull of its size duly led one arranger to make it the ultimate goal in a literal, ricocheting pinball journey, using a pea and a rubber band. The stand, however, was also imagined in a range of other ways: as a stage for talks, as a collective for small publishers, as a bookstore or as the toilets. Our shiny silver stand was also accorded several different functions – from publisher services, to a new digital publisher, to the entrance point, to toilets (again). This attention to outliers and unusual stands, we suggest, shows a tendency towards seeing and celebrating variety and new creative possibilities in the industry, expressed here through a differentiated physical environment.

Third, the corporate feel of the model also provoked commentary. One person narrativised a typical trade fair experience: 'This is where you come in and you get your program and your lanyard. It's designed so you can do a full circuit and see everything. Here's where you can cut across and meet your friends.' A second person suggested that this was 'kinda like IKEA' and the first agreed, 'yes, you can't get out.' A third participant was reminded of the time they worked in corporate communications and attended annual AGMs, suggesting that the arrangement of stands felt generically corporate and therefore not specific to the book industry. The absence of the visual markers of bookishness in our model revealed in our participants' narratives the underlying corporate aspects of the publishing industry. Focusing upon the materials and dimensions of the stands as communicative devices stripped away the language of a very textual industry in order to expose its habitus.

So much for the public presentation of space at the Frankfurter Buchmesse. What's happening behind the scenes? In Chapter 1 we examined how buzz circulates and builds in informal spaces. In the second section of this chapter we explore what an intensive investigation of these spaces reveals about the deeper dynamics of the Fair.

Behind the Scenes: Private and Informal Spaces

In 2018 we took a trip to the toilets in Hall 6.2 and discovered a world behind the scenes of the Buchmesse. Once past the Google Play stand, we opened a door and entered a hauntingly empty space lined by the reverse of publishers' stands on one side and the entrance to the toilets on the other (see Figure 8). A wall of windows at one end opened out into a view of the Messe's other buildings, some no longer used for the Fair. In the middle were tumbleweeds, echoes and emptiness.

Figure 8 Behind the scenes at the Buchmesse

In this section of this chapter we consider the less public face of the Buchmesse. We explore non-displays and quietness, shrinking space and emptiness. And we look at informal spaces accessible only through dérives, happenstance and privilege.

Non-displays, Hidden and Transient Spaces

Some things aren't visible at the Buchmesse. Many publishers can't afford to travel there at all, especially those located at a distance from Europe, such as African, Australian, Indian and Chinese publishers. Some can afford to get to Frankfurt and buy a trade visitor ticket, but have no stand. When we spoke to Eloise Millar from Galley Beggar Press (as discussed in Chapter 1, a remarkably successful small publisher) about our interest in using a laser to measure stands, she responded, 'you'll have to measure me.' Her body was the closest thing to a stand she had. Our interview with her, which discussed the 900-page experimental book that made the Booker Prize shortlist (*Ducks, Newburyport*), was held at a café table. Others hold meetings in hotels, chairs in the hallways or benches in the agora. An army of foot soldiers travels from stand to stand, meeting others on their territory and requiring those comfortable shoes.

That small publishers continue to attend the Buchmesse relates to its earlier, contested history, which is examined further in Chapter 3. As Niemeier (2001) explains, during the 1970s and 1980s a number of 'Gegenbuchmessen' – alternative, counter book fairs – took place, mostly organised by left-leaning publishers who rejected the 'author mills' and strategic marketing of bestsellers they saw as dominating the Buchmesse (for example, higher marketing spending, promoting authors as stars and cross-media strategies). These Gegenbuchmessen were sometimes controversial and sometimes supported – one received funding from the City of Frankfurt. But in 1984 the Frankfurt Book Fair offered small publishers cheaper rates and the option of joint stalls, and most of them came back to the Buchmesse.

Not all non-displays of power are the result of budget constraints. Some powerful companies engage in strategic non-displays. Staff from Netflix, YouTube and Nintendo – game changers in the media industries – were present at the Fair but did not have stands. Instead, they operated under the radar in a shadow network of meetings in interstitial locations. At these meetings, as far as we could tell, ordinary business took place: the pitching of content to be acquired, discussions about co-licensing arrangements and soft social encounters. These cross-media meetings have a growing financial significance and play a role in generating buzz, but are yet to form a highly visible component of the Fair. Breaking through this invisibility in 2019, Netflix's vice president of international originals, Kelly Luegenbiehl, was a speaker at the high-profile Global 50 CEO Talk (Nawotka 2019b). The company thus assumed a significant and highly visible space on the programme, if not in the halls.

Throughout our fieldwork, due to our method of the dérive and our mischievousness, we were also intrigued by hidden and transient spaces. We extended our explorations outside the ticketed space of the Fair itself to informal locations such as hotels and parties, and even to chance meetings on planes to and from the Buchmesse. We inserted ourselves bodily into such situations, our own physical presences in these off-site locations enabling our observations, involvements and occasional interventions.

We learned of and then witnessed pre-meetings at the Frankfurter and Hessischer Hofs on the Monday and Tuesday of Fair week, as well as meetings there throughout the Fair.[9] The drinks which extend from the early evening into the night at the same two hotels are an off-site institution which we explore further in Chapter 3, along with parties more generally.

At the Fair itself the Business Club is marketed as an exclusive area or, as detailed in the Buchmesse's copy, a 'full-service meeting niche reserved exclusively for your company inside the Business Club – with the added bonus of boosting your visibility among the publishing elite . . . away from the hectic atmosphere of the fair' (Frankfurter Buchmesse 2019b). We were signed in by friends (and ended up lightly satirising the space as the 'Executive Club' in Blaire Squiscoll's *The Frankfurt Kabuff* (2019a)), but other contacts, secure in their own publisher stands, told us nothing happens there. On our entry we found groupings of international publishers and journalists, brought together as 'Business Club Ambassadors' (Frankfurter Buchmesse 2019d), including people from Argentina, Brazil and India, as well as Australia, the USA and the UK. Several publishers (though not German ones) also told us nothing happens at the weekend and indeed many fly home on the Friday. From the international publishers' perspective, the perceived non-activity at the weekend is another kind of emptiness and non-display. However, for the public and the German publishers, as Chapter 3 explores further, these days matter.

Then, our eyes drawn by our measuring activity, we started noticing cupboards. Dubbed 'Kabuffs' by German publishers, a word akin to the English 'closet' in its metaphorical resonances, these cupboards were sometimes low down, tucked under benches, sometimes the size of a small room, accessed through a door (often with a porthole). We asked if we could look inside some and were granted puzzled, occasionally proud, guided tours.

[9] Grammatically correct German would be *die Höfe*, but anglophone publishers commonly use 'the Hofs'.

Cupboards are essential to the behind-the-scenes logistics of publishing stands, we learned, storing food (including canapés), drink and medicines, and they also contributed to the development of the Frankfurt Kabuff.

Our dériving also showed the impact of the distances between halls and stands. We found as suspected that not everyone walks the halls, and so the advice to wear comfortable shoes was not relevant to all. The spaces of the Fair are practically inaccessible to some, for example, one contact who was stuck in back-to-back half hour meetings and could only occasionally escape for fresh air, food or a toilet break. On the other hand, the transient spaces are all that is accessible to those who lack the funds to purchase stand space of their own. It was on escalators that we clocked the sartorial dominance of blue suits, that we looked down at people signing the Freedom of Speech wall, and that we overhead snatches of conversation. It was also on escalators and stairs that we confronted our lostness several times, trying to work out what floor of what hall we were on.

One particular moment during our fieldwork was indicative of the nature of our dérives in hidden spaces. With a group of around half a dozen colleagues we got lost on the way from Hall 6 to an off-site party. While we drifted down a staircase we took the opportunity to conduct an additional research interview; in an open space we participated in a long discussion about how the hall we found ourselves next to had formerly housed publisher stands. Some international bonding occurred and – once we had found ourselves again – we introduced our contacts to the Situationist International as a way of framing being lost in a way which produced grounded and engaged knowledge. Fleeting moments such as these are not normally recounted in academic or industry narratives about the Buchmesse, and might seem trivial. We argue that they reflect the lived reality of the Fair and give insight into how the Fair's behind-the-scenes spaces complement its more obvious operations.

Shrinking, Negative Space and the Publisher's Stand Reversed

What about negative space? As mentioned earlier, we noted a blank area behind stands in Hall 6 and our questions about it led to people telling us about the Fair's size reduction in recent years. In fact, in every year of our fieldwork people told us the Fair was smaller than the year before (we increasingly started to wonder if it exists at all). They also told us their memories of the International Hall being located in the no longer used Hall 8. The footprint of the Fair is shrinking on the Messe site. A ghost or shadow Buchmesse exists in the mind of long-term attendees who remember when the Fair – and, they imply by metaphorical extension, the industry – was bigger.

Such negative space and the mood of the Fair are linked. A memory of formerly large, bustling spaces (which we term 'megativity') informs one of the negative moods which impedes the production of buzz, as detailed in our typology in Chapter 1.[10] Negativity is a familiar mood in publishing, which, as we note in the introduction, is powered by existential crisis. Accounts that reflect in elegiac mode on the diminution of the Fair render this mood evident. As one blogger wrote:

> In my early years in publishing, the Frankfurt Book Fair was
> the most exciting place I could imagine, but over the decades
> my fascination for it waned ... A lot of publicity is gener-
> ated during the fair as well, but as a publisher, you are no
> longer obliged to go there, nor do you risk your credibility
> and sales by not going. Last year (2013) was my final book
> fair after 31 years. There were many empty booths (meaning
> publishers who reserved a booth simply did not appear) and
> a lot of unused space behind the aisles in some of the halls.
> All of my friends whom I met at the fair agreed that there
> were significantly fewer professional visitors than in the
> years before. (Hartmann 2014)

This persistent mood (the Fair always feels smaller) is borne out, in recent years, by reality – the Fair actually is smaller. The disruptions to Frankfurt and the traditional book industry are real. As noted earlier, some of the most significant actors are media companies that operate invisibly, hold meetings underground (not literally) or otherwise obscure the size of their influence.

---

[10] We discuss 'megativity' and 'miniaturisation' in greater detail in Driscoll and Squires (2020c).

Figure 9 Publisher's Stand Reversed with uninvited visitors

A sense of loss and threat balances the boosterism of media reports about Frankfurt, a negativity that operates in counterpoint to the scale and bustle of the Fair's 'megativity'. In Hall 6 the vast empty space between the stands and the toilets is, perhaps, the repressed unconscious of the Fair, the space where the secrets of industry failure hide behind confident pronouncements and the bold face of buzzness as usual and growth growth growth. The sudden transition from bustling hall floor to dead zone made us contemplate industry retraction, the global economy and the various costs – including those of environmental sustainability, as discussed earlier – of such large events.

The hidden zone in Hall 6 inspired us to set up a Publisher's Stand Reversed in 2019 (see Figure 9). We noticed a nook formed by the reverse of panels from a legitimate stand, and two chairs nearby. We dragged these into the nook and placed a copy of our self-published autoethnographic comic erotic thriller, *The Frankfurt Kabuff* (Squiscoll 2019a), prominently between some plaster offcuts. At first we simply sat and relished the quiet of the space and the respite from constant socialising. The Buchmesse is full of people seeking an opportunity to privately collect their thoughts (we later noted others using the hidden zone for moments of rest). Soon we commenced Ullapoolist activity. We read through the industry newsletters we had collected and began ripping out words to form collages that represented each day – a key step in our processing of buzz generation at Frankfurt, as discussed in Chapter 1. We fell short of arranging meetings at 'our' stand (although we were tempted, especially at the thought of giving directions to people), but continued to use it every day of the Fair, a ritual of belonging and attachment that reflectively activated the Buchmesse's negative spaces.

Conclusion

Our observations of the Buchmesse, gathered in accordance with our situationist, autoethnographic epistemology and our experimental methods, offer a new vantage point on the Fair. The sensing-thinking-doing epistemology of Ullapoolism yields situated knowledge of how the Buchmesse as a physical site in contemporary publishing and book culture affects the circulation of people and content. The dérives we undertook in 2017, 2018 and 2019 revealed the impact of the physical structures of the Fair: how outsized stands in central positions reinforce the market dominance of multinational publishers; how small publishers struggle for visibility and try to build alliances; how the costs of travel in terms of exhaustion, effort and economic outlay, disadvantage some.

The Cardboard Buchmesse, a détournement of the Fair, was a dynamic, interactive intervention that combined participant observation and situationist, low theory dérives with an arts-informed 'make and do' project. Through its construction we developed knowledge of how the Fair shapes the publishing industry, and we made a critical intervention that probed beneath industry commonplaces about shoes and the size of the Fair. In so doing, we investigated the significance of position, size and structure of the physical environments of the Buchmesse, their effects upon the networks of the publishing industry and the resulting trajectories of people and books through those networks. The Cardboard Buchmesse highlighted contrasts within the industry and the corporate aspects that sit alongside bookishness. As a creative method it moved beyond fixed scholarly models of power relations (such as those of Bourdieu) to imagine new relations and new features, understanding not just what the Fair is, but also what it might be.

Just as importantly, our attention to the invisible, transient, hidden and negative spaces of the Fair underscores the underlying dynamics and uneasy tensions embedded within the ecologies of neoliberal publishing. The Publisher's Stand Reversed was both a reprieve from the Fair and an encounter with its shrinking footprint and wasteful underside: loose cables, discarded chairs, paper rubbish. The exploration of Kabuffs revealed the mundane work that sustains the buzzy glamour of publishing and good news stories about future bestsellers: coat and bag storage, supplies, mess, walls that fall down and need to be taped up again. Our interest in interstitial, on-the-way, hidden spaces and cupboards also led us to write *The Frankfurt Kabuff* (Squiscoll 2019a) in order to develop our observations in creative form. The novella also taps into the carnivalesque, as explored in the next chapter.

Our investigative practices and imaginative forays, then, instances of 'low theory' in action, give depth to understanding of how buzz is produced at Frankfurt. There is a link between the size and shape of the Fair and its mood: the advice to wear comfortable shoes sends a message about the market share of the publishing industry. There are also, we discovered, aspects of the physicality of the Fair that communicate obstacles and challenges of the publishing industry: cost, wasteful production and pathways that are blocked, inaccessible or exclusionary. Through this chapter we have demonstrated how the physical construction of the Buchmesse and the behaviours it creates serve to replicate global industry structures, as well as metaphorically to reinforce them.

3 Carnivalesque

'COME ON IN! JOIN THE FUN!' – Visit the Bhil Carnival
(Amaliyar and Wolf 2015)

We're in Hall 4.0 acquiring bullet journals, a hardback bound paper tool we
use as researchers for organising ourselves. We take advantage of
Leuchtturm's free monogramming offer, adding the initials NU NU and
OT OT to our books. Nunu and Otot, as we write elsewhere (Driscoll and
Squires 2020a), are little wormlike creatures that animate our Ullapoolist
slogan, 'No Insight with Inside, No Inside without Outside'. They are
another key mode for our conceptual approach to the inside and outside of
bookish events – defined through physical as well as sociopolitical inclu-
sions and exclusions – and are particularly relevant to this chapter focusing
on the carnivalesque aspects of the Frankfurter Buchmesse.

A queue has gathered for the monogramming services, so we leave our
bullet journals to pick up later and investigate the rest of the hall. It's full of
what a sign tells us are NON-BOOK, or rather book-adjacent products:
pens, stamps and ink pads, notebooks and greeting cards. There are
companies that produce impressive feats of paper engineering; dioramas,
pop-up and lift-the-flap books that take the codex beyond the rectangular
into the multidimensional.

We stop at the Tara Arts stand and one of us buys a copy of *Visit the Bhil
Carnival* by Subhash Amaliyar and Gita Wolf.[11] 'Neela and Peela are off to
the fair,' starts the book. 'Come in.' Inside the hardcovers of the book is
a fold-out sheet which reveals an Indian village carnival and a tiny inset
book of 'Stories'. 'The place is busy! They see lots of happy people meeting
friends, drinking, eating, and playing' (Amaliyar and Wolf 2015).[12]

---

[11] We note this purchase – as of the notebooks – was on a THURSDAY. We
discuss the rules pertaining to how and when books can be sold at the Buchmesse
later in this chapter, and remain uncertain as to whether a different rule operates
for non-book goods and pop-up books.

[12] It is very hard to reference exact locations in this book object.

This description of the Bhil carnival might also suit the Buchmesse, a recurrent event at which people from around the book world happily gather to meet friends, drink, eat, play, exchange international rights and generate bestsellers. Analyses of contemporary cultural festivals draw on ideas of the carnival to articulate their periodic, playful and out-of-the ordinary aspects while acknowledging that the festivals tend to promote the creative economy rather than create a concerted sense of a world turned upside down (see Arcordia and Whitford 2006). But can Frankfurt's convivial, social and even excessive practices be read as carnivalesque? And how would such a reading marry with the role of the Buchmesse as a market-oriented trade fair with its primary goal – albeit achieved via human interconnection – the exchange of capital and copyright and the generation of global bestsellers?

Moeran puts forward the idea that book trade fairs – at least in their 'boozy' parties and other instances of sociality – have a carnivalesque aspect to them (Moeran 2011, 87). This aspect, he argues, is an extension of the historical relationship that can be drawn between the mediaeval fair and its latter-day instantiations such as the Buchmesse that equate 'fair time' with 'carnival time' (2011, 87). Moeran's thinking builds on Appadurai's conceptualisation of tournaments of value as '"complex periodic events that are removed in some culturally well defined way from the routine of everyday economic life. Participation in them is ... both a privilege for those in power and an instrument of status contests between them"' (1986, 21, cited in Moeran 2011, 138).

The mediaeval version of the carnival, particularly as theorised by Bakhtin in its literary form as the carnivalesque, is a radically disruptive space containing within it 'free and familiar contact between people' and 'a new mode of interrelationships between individuals', 'eccentricity', 'carnivalistic mésalliances' and 'profanation', all of which undermine the sacred and emphasise the bodily (Bakhtin 1984, 122–3). These forms of resistance merge the aesthetic and the political, but – sanctioned by the state or the church, or in modern versions the forces of global capital – also operate as periodic 'safety valves' before a return to everyday life. In contrast, a situationist account of carnival instead sees it as a moment of revolutionary potential, a force which turns spectacular capitalism against itself (Grindon 2004), and thus as a moment which instils the revolutionary into everyday life (to adapt the title of situationist Raoul Vaneigem's 1967 book, *The Revolution of Everyday Life* (Vaneigem 2001) as well as to 'fair time'.

Is the Buchmesse either of these two versions of the carnival? Or does a somewhat looser badge apply describing the festive, often drink-fuelled, sometimes excessive sociality of this periodic global gathering? It is unlikely that the organisers of the Buchmesse construct their event as disruptive to the publishing industry or the forces of global capitalism, or as holding true revolutionary potential. However, following Moeran's claim that 'the contingency of personal interaction, the lightness of "talk" and the carnival-like setting of fairs make them a site where disorder might be created that in turn can lead to change of field and market' (Moeran 2011, abstract), in this chapter we take three approaches. First, we create a space through which to examine the carnivalesque aspects of the Fair (parties, sociality, after-hours events), especially in relation to their potential for excessive and even abusive behaviours. Second, we analyse the challenging and disruptive geopolitical aspects of the Fair including through an excavatory examination of its historical development. Finally, we think through what carnivalesque – and perhaps incendiary – interventions by scholar-participants at the Buchmesse might look like.

Methods and Musical Accompaniments

Following the pattern of our previous chapters, this chapter draws on a range of creative and critical methods to examine the Buchmesse via the carnivalesque. In addition to industry accounts of the social and political aspects of the Buchmesse, our methods include our autoethnographic attendance at parties to which we were invited, paused at en route to somewhere else or gatecrashed (a time-worn method of party attendance at Frankfurt). Our mode was as participant-observers, but given the typical environment of parties our participation involved full bodily immersion: lipstick and party frocks and consumption of alcohol and canapés. As we detail later, some of this activity confirmed our observations about the gendered and occasional sleazy nature of the Buchmesse, which resulted in our creation of the 'Sleaze-O-Meter'. As a research mode, it also threw up questions about the ethical challenges of auto-ethnographic research when it requires researchers to be fully immersed in an environment, encounter questionable or even abusive behaviours and use their own bodies in the creation of research findings and pursuit of situations.

These observations, alongside findings from our other creative research methods, led us to create a fictional account of the Fair in *The Frankfurt Kabuff*, as we discussed in Chapter 2. Featuring imagined and very lightly fictionalised versions of Buchmesse parties (with accompanying Spotify playlists), the novella examines geopolitical and gender dynamics at the Fair in ways in which a Cambridge University Press minigraph might shy away from (e.g., sex scenes). Much of this chapter might usefully be read alongside the novella, as its imaginative approach to the Buchmesse is as much a research output as this current book.[13] Similarly this chapter, following the promptings of both *Visit the Bhil Carnival* and *The Frankfurt Kabuff*, includes inserted stories, playlists, metaphorical pop-ups and musings on further, non-actualised carnivalesque interventions.

Parties and Playlists

The German concept of 'Frankfurt Fieber' (fever) casts the whole Buchmesse as a party, both entertainment and a consolation for the gloom of everyday life (Niemeier 2001, 116). The official 2019 app for the Buchmesse includes, under its 'Recommendations from Insiders', a 'Buchmesse Party-Guide' illustrated by a nightclub scene. 'During the Frankfurter Buchmesse the nightlife pulsates,' claims the app, with suggested off-site events to attend.

The industry dailies produced during the Fair (and détourned as collages for Chapter 1) also accentuate partying as a key behaviour. *The Bookseller*'s 'My Frankfurt Book Fair' column, for example, sees interviewees prompted by and eagerly responding to questions about Buchmesse partying. 'The drinks parties on the Tuesday when everyone is fresh faced are always fun.

[13] We note our intention to produce a critical edition of *The Frankfurt Kabuff* and are happy to receive offers from any publisher reading this footnote.

However, they do come with their dangers . . . my main tip to survive the fair is don't party too hard on the first day, unless you're superhuman (which admittedly a good few publishing people seem to be during fair week)' (Ricchetti 2019). The same feature the following day had its contributor talking about 'the best party I've been to at FBF': 'I don't know if you'd really call it a party, but it was 5am on the Saturday morning, in the very brightly-lit cigar room in the Hof. A scout, two other agents and I were dancing to YouTube videos of 1990s rap on a phone' (Tivnan 2019). The same year *The Bookseller*'s satirical, pseudonymous diarist 'Horace Bent' reported on the 'vicious scrum' at the Frankfurter Hof bar (Bent 2019). The previous day the columnist had turned his sights to the Hessischer Hof's 'must-attend' Hachette party and the tendency of book industry people (Bent included, he implies) to turn up 'without RSVP'ing' (Bent 2019).

Such a snapshot of media accounts of parties immediately gives a flavour of Frankfurt's out-of-hours culture. Yet, as our own experiences showed us, the partying starts earlier in the day and within the Buchmesse site itself, with stand parties held either to promote a particular activity (for example, Amazon Crossing's 2019 logo launch, discussed in Chapter 1) or as well-established and expected events often hosted by national agencies. Our trajectories through the Buchmesse in 2017, 2018 and 2019 took us to many of these events, which as well as welcoming business partners, friends and random passers-by also utilise national products in the construction of their identities: caipirinhas at the Brazilian Publishers stand, Guinness and live folk music at Publishing Ireland, beers at the Australian Publishing Association and whisky and craft gin at Publishing Scotland (in addition to the standardised Buchmesse canapés ordered via official caterers).[14] Stand parties tend to operate without speeches, although there might be a cake cutting to mark a special occasion (Publishing Scotland's forty-fifth anniversary, for example), or a political intervention, such as the Irish ambassador to Germany's

---

[14] An inexhaustive list of Frankfurt snacks includes Apfelwein, Kartoffelsalat, pizza, wood-fired salmon, goat cheese tarts, toast with meat spread, lollies, sausage rolls, sausages, vegemite on toast, cheese and crackers, cake, potato crisps/chips and ice cream.

mention of his country's strong identity as a European nation in 2018 (in the context of, but without once referencing, the UK's Brexit vote).

After three years of attending stand parties, we recognised and participated in a ritualistic approach to these events: Thursday afternoon moving from the joint Australia and UK Independent Publishers Guild party at 5.30 PM, to Publishing Scotland (also at 5.30 PM), Friday from Ireland at 5.00 PM to New Zealand at about 6.00 PM. Our party trajectories were inevitably inflected by our anglophone networks as well as the proximity of these parties on different levels of the same hall. The annual pattern creates a sense of familiarity and of cyclical time. Individuals catch up on their contacts' news, both professional and personal: a job move, searching for work, a child, illness, divorce, a new partner (similar patterns of personal and professional information sharing in business meetings are discussed in Chapter 1 and by Moeran (2011), but here with the addition of alcohol). They might also have conversations about market conditions and international politics. Our research methods did not include network maps of attendance at these parties, but to do so would undoubtedly reveal (in addition to the random passers-by drawn in by the free food and drink) affinities formed through national, geopolitical and linguistic groupings or forged through translation deals, and intercultural bonds created by schemes such as Publishing Scotland's Publishing Fellowship and the Australia Council's similar Visiting International Publisher scheme (which bring publishers from around the world to their respective countries in order to generate and boost rights sales). There are insiders and outsiders even at these apparently open stand parties: whether through invitations and RSVPs (not enforced, as far as we could tell), knowledge of when and where the parties would be or familiarity with other attendees. The parties balance the marketing of national industry in order to gather new rights business with fostering a sense of belonging and attachment for attendees.

The typology of Frankfurt parties also includes 'family' dinners (for small groups of staff working at the same company, typically held early on in the Fair), author dinners hosted by literary agencies with international publishing partners and big publisher parties offsite hosted both by German and by international publishers, as well as nightly gatherings in 'the Hofs'.

One of the most concerted accounts of partying at Frankfurt appeared in a lengthy *Harper's* magazine article by Gideon Lewis-Kraus in 2009. Over several days and nights Lewis-Kraus traversed the dealmaking, networking and socialising sites of Frankfurt during the Buchmesse – an environment a more intentionally satirical account called 'a traditionally ribald and booze-sodden week every October' (Gould 2007). His account of parties attended included early morning champagne consumption by the US publisher of that year's just-announced Booker Prize winner, which sneaked in some national stereotypes: 'At the Russian and French and Italian booths the wine is opened circa 09h00, but when the American managerial establishment pops a cork there's got to be a reason for it' (Lewis-Kraus 2009, 49).

Lewis-Kraus encounters FOMO and actual MO (see Chapter 1 for further accounts of FOMO) when another journalist quizzes him as to whether he made it to 'the big HarperCollins party for Paulo Coelho'; he hadn't, to which Mokoto Rich responded that 'it's a shame I didn't go, because it "was such ridiculous theater" and "would have made really great material"' for his article (Lewis-Kraus 2009, 48). This journalistic one-up (wo)manship links to Moeran's (2010, 148) observation of the role of Frankfurt parties in creating insider and outsider status.

In mitigation for missing the HarperCollins party, Lewis-Kraus tells Rich that he was at another 'exclusive' dinner populated by 'a dozen of the more stylish international publishers' (Lewis-Kraus 2009, 45) brought together by the Wylie Agency in honour of Eli Horowitz of US publisher McSweeneys and at which the Booker Prize winner's UK editor arrives hot foot from London celebrations. The Booker Prize, which is often announced in the same week as the Buchmesse (we watched the livestream of the 2019 ceremony from our hotel room, in which the shortlisted *Ducks, Newburyport* discussed in Chapter 1 lost out to controversially awarded joint winners), provided recurring moments of buzz in Lewis-Kraus' article. Various international editors and publishers celebrated their connections to the winner, whether it was in the early morning popping of a champagne cork or beyond midnight bottles of wine. For one US publisher in Lewis-Kraus' account it was his third Booker winner in a row, a pattern of success that affirmed his identity as 'the industry's boulevardier' (46), one of the high prestige, man-about-town publishers of literary fiction. Such moments of celebration are post-publication versions of buzz, occurring long after the initial deals, but they are used to promote further rights sales. Celebrations also cement the social aspects of the Fair forged through the bringing together of rights sales and taste, as one Dutch publisher explains to Lewis-Kraus: 'It's being here with my soul brothers and soul sisters . . . These are people who have the same tastes, who like the same books' (45) Such non-competitive international 'familial relationship[s]' demonstrate 'personal intimacy' as 'evidence of, and a vehicle for, the broader potential of translatability; the friendships' which 'enact the international market' (43).

Partying, then, is a crucial element of Buchmesse buzzness: for companies and individuals to throw or attend the hottest parties, to assert various forms of cool identity, and to forge international relationships, both professional and personal. Realising the centrality to the Fair of parties, *The Frankfurt Kabuff* (itself launched at multiple pop-up parties in 2019) features two parties as well as drinks receptions (replete with canapés) as part of its narrative. The heroine, Beatrice Deft, attends a party in a nightclub situated off an insalubrious, piss-smelling alley. What follows is a tiny, inset section of that narrative:

> A dark-haired Frankfurter at the door gave her a quick glance and ushered her in. She found herself walking along a crimson corridor, surrounded by erotic art. She followed it to a steep staircase, into a womb-like space below. In the tiny dark room, Primal Scream's 'Loaded' blasted from tinny speakers. Beatrice was unexpectedly charmed. Everywhere she looked, suited men and chicly dressed women smiled, talked, and bobbed along to the music. Genuine enthusiasm animated their gestures and expressions. Once, she had been this optimistic. She wondered if she could be again. (Squiscoll 2019a, 6–7)

The scene, juxtaposed with Beatrice's ennui, lightly references both a trope of genre fiction (the alienated, damaged protagonist) and the publishing industry's collective sense of belief and positivity.

At *The Frankfurt Kabuff* party is a happily dancing ambassador who 'loves books. And parties' (Squiscoll 2019a, 10), and – more important for the plot – discussion of 'an attack, bombs, at the Book Fair' (9). This imaginative reworking by our author alter ego of a publisher's party we attended in 2018 also has an accompanying Spotify playlist (Squiscoll 2019b), created from autoethnographically half-remembered music played by a DJ-publisher. Such 'notorious' parties (in this case, Canongate's; Gould 2007) create their own sense of buzz around the 'cool' publishers or literary agencies, rather than around individual books or their authors, as they extend late into the night.

So while not everyone at Frankfurt parties hard (as noted in Chapter 1), it is no wonder that when we were allowed to look into publishers' Kabuffs (as detailed in Chapter 2) we found, as well as bottles of Sekt, beer and wine, the medicines Alka Seltzer and Berocca, taken for their curative post-hangover properties. A hangover of a different magnitude is prefigured by Lewis-Kraus' contextualisation of the publishing industry's constant sense of 'apocalypse' (Lewis-Kraus 2009, 41), as discussed by us throughout this book. Lewis-Kraus' article's title, 'The Last Book Party', refers to 'probably the last big Bertelsmann party' hosted by the German publishing group (50). Indeed, informal discussions in 2017–19 indicated to us that German publishers had cut down on the number of parties (including the Bertelsmann party), thereby reducing 'Frankfurt Fieber'. Parties expand and contract with the economic health of the industry, an index of its mood. Frankfurt's carnivalesque atmosphere of excessive sociality also presents a range of challenges that speak to the industry's deeper dynamics, as the next section of this chapter investigates.

Politics and Power

Parties and politics might seem an odd conjoining of topics for this final, carnivalesque chapter, but insider and outsider status, as the previous section outlined, are constructed via party invitation and attendance and are intimately linked to the circles of influence and power at the Buchmesse. This section of this chapter examines aspects of sex, sleaze and gender, national groupings and stereotypes, and the Buchmesse's disruptive politics from the 1960s to the present day.

Sex, Sleaze and Gender

The excessive sociality of the Buchmesse also links to its libidinality. Lewis-Kraus' article is replete with anecdotes of affairs starting in the public rooms of 'the Hofs' before transferring to more private rooms, as well as including the oft-repeated story that sex workers are less busy during Frankfurt because 'the publishers all sleep with one another' (Lewis-Kraus 2009, 45) (a story told to us in various forms during our visits to Frankfurt, sometimes to distinguish the Buchmesse from the big car show held biannually in Frankfurt until 2019). Gould's satirical account of the Buchmesse, 'No One Got Naked at the Frankfurt Book Fair' (Gould 2007), the title of which is a reference to one publisher's predilection for 'DJ-ing and occasionally disrobing', ends up mocking the 'usual suspects' partying until the small hours with a dismissive put-down. 'That is just sad at this point. It's not 1987 anymore, or even 1997. Go home to your wives!' Gould points implicitly to the gendered aspect of Frankfurt partying.

On our arrival at the Buchmesse in 2017, in the immediate aftermath of the revelations about Harvey Weinstein (see Cobb and Horeck 2018; Boyle 2019), and as part of our observational research methods, we noted the gendered aspects of the Fair. At the alcohol-fuelled stand parties we attended we noticed lots of young women in colourful dresses and older men in suits, as well as multiple moments of sleaze across the halls as men looked women up and down and took advantage of their captive positions on stands to talk at them for extended periods – a casual appropriation of women's bodies and attention. In Hall 6 an elderly American publisher asked one of us if she had dated him in the past. The following year bestselling author Anna Todd and fellow female authors, publishers and agents were harassed by a group of men in a Frankfurt hotel bar. Her video of the incident went viral on Twitter and – fearful of further encounters with the men – she cancelled her appearance at the Buchmesse (Rahman 2018).

As we discuss in our article 'The Sleaze-O-Meter: Sexual Harassment in the Publishing Industry' (Squires and Driscoll 2018), our observations fitted with a broader set of abusive and harassing behaviours in the publishing industry. The industry's events-based culture, involving substantial work after hours, often with alcohol, increases risk. In the United States, one editor discussed the historical foundations of the link between publishing's social nature and abusive behaviour stemming from the 'industry's reputation as a place where anything goes, which adds to the glamour of the business' (Deahl, Maher and Milliot 2017).

The conviviality of the publishing industry is tied to its abusive behaviours. Book fairs, literary festivals and other book-based events away from the office are often constructed as an attractive aspect of the job, but for a respondent to an Australian survey 'event settings are where harassment is most likely to occur . . . Book publishing, as a social industry with lots of launches and public readings, lends itself to these kinds of abuse with little accountability' (Books+Publishing 2017). This version of the carnivalesque reasserts masculine forms of power rather than upturning them. In order to combat these behaviours we conceptualised and then brought into scholarly direct action in 2018 the Sleaze-O-Meter, an old-fashioned tally counter used to click after each mansplain or leer at the Buchmesse.

National Groupings, Stereotypes and Racism

As the previous two chapters of this book have unfolded, the Buchmesse to a certain degree replicates and also works actively to construct the shape of the global publishing industry. Its halls and aisles are organised along national and linguistic grounds, as Chapter 2 discusses, and the meetings between members of the book industry work towards cementing various kinds of affiliation as well as extending transnational partnerships. The Fair aims to present the harmonious operations of the global industry, one in which cosmopolitan, bookish discourse and international commerce are foregrounded. Just as parties create insiders and outsiders, however, the Fair's physical groupings create lines of inclusion and exclusion, along with moments of national stereotyping, neocolonial practices and even racism, which conjoin with the sleazy and harassing behaviours discussed in the previous section.

The self-presentation of national book agencies and publishers' associations at the Buchmesse, as our investigations at parties revealed, frequently draws on national (non-book) products and stereotypes. These stereotypes, while chosen by the agencies and organisations themselves, can nonetheless be linked to the tropes used across the global publishing industry in the categorisations and marketing of national, regional, ethnic, religious or other forms of identity (see Huggan 2001; Brouillette 2007; Squires 2007; Chambers 2010; Saha 2016). The various iterations of the guest of honour at Frankfurt, as discussed later in this chapter, also reveal self-constructions of literary and cultural identity mediated by the Buchmesse.

As discussed in Chapter 2, Frankfurt's halls are arranged along geographical lines which map onto different territorial markets for both the buying and selling of rights. The differential market power of these regions is expressed in social interactions at the Fair. One of the focal points of Gonsalves' research at Frankfurt, discussed in Chapter 2, was the efforts of her Indian interviewees to feel accepted at the Buchmesse. Reading her interviewees' strategies through the lens of 'friendliness', Gonsalves depicts an independent publisher using such approaches to attempt entry literally into the UK/US hall (during her research period, Hall 8) and figuratively into bigger business opportunities. For this interviewee and her 'collective' it was important 'to be recognised as "worthy" of being in Hall 8' (Gonsalves 2015, 440). For Gonsalves her interviewee's strategies did not align with Bourdieusian conceptualisations of newcomers needing to aim for 'discontinuity, rupture, difference, revolution' (Bourdieu 1993, 106), but instead were about wanting to be 'accepted by the establishment, and being seen as fit enough to be admissible into the prestigious Hall 8' (Gonsalves 2015, 440). Given the context of the racist commentary in the press about India's designation as guest of honour in 1986 and again in 2006, such a strategy is understandable (Richard 2006; Knapp 2007). That such a strategy is required shows the Fair reinforcing rather than mitigating against the established power relations of the publishing industry.

Gonsalves' findings intersect with those of Longley (in Treglown and Bennett 1998) in her discussion of Ireland as guest of honour at Frankfurt in 1996. She perceives in the programme an abasement, lacking in confrontational ambition, towards the global book markets which is simultaneously self-fashioned and externally constructed through national stereotypes.

As Longley describes, 'Frankfurt was about national self-image as well as about selling international rights', and in a Frankfurt edition of *Books Ireland*, a German publisher articulated 'the German "enthusiasm" for Ireland in a manner that suggests . . . the potential and danger of the literary export market as it influences critical reception' (Treglown and Bennett 1998, 213). The German publisher said:

> It seems to date back to a romanticised and idealist
> nineteenth-century image of the Emerald Isle as symbolising
> everything noble and good. Add to this the experience of an
> oppressed and enslaved [*sic*] people and there is the recipe
> for sympathy and solidarity. Peace-loving and innocent, the
> Irish are seen as devoid of any ambition to dominate world
> politics, and their heroes fight with words rather than
> swords. (cited in Treglown and Bennett 1998, 213)

For more 'peripheral' literary cultures the 'potential and danger' of Frankfurt attendance, as Longley sees it, includes both the exoticising tendencies of 'critical reception' and marketing, and the need for the smaller, newer markets to conform to the behavioural patterns of the more powerful, established ones. This is not carnival as disruptive or as revolutionary, but as a performance that re-inscribes existing inequalities.

The Buchmesse and 1960s Politics

A tension between disruption and conservative re-inscriptions of order is thus built into the modern Buchmesse. The construction of the Buchmesse as the go-to destination for the global book industry was actively tied to the Fair's historical development within regional, national and indeed international politics. This section therefore takes on an excavatory mode in order to bring aspects of the Buchmesse's past into a critical understanding of its present.

Historical accounts of the Buchmesse describe its role in the post-war reconstruction of Germany, with its 1948 iteration as the 'Bücherplatz Frankfurt' exhibition marking a new beginning. Initially Frankfurt competed with other cities (including Hamburg and Stuttgart) to become the pre-eminent West German book fair. Frankfurt was deemed the most suitable location because of its geographical placement at the intersection of the Western Zones (as well as its longer historical legacy). In 1949 a fair element organised by booksellers and publishers was added to the exhibition, with the public permitted to enter (Seyer 2007, 163–4). This fair was located at the Paulskirche, a historically important site for German democracy: the location of the first unified German parliament in 1848, and the first building reconstructed after the heavy war-time bombing of Frankfurt. The post-war rise of Frankfurt as the city of the book business was simultaneous with the city's development as the centre of German and indeed European finance.

From 1950 the Börsenverein des Deutschen Buchhandels (German Publishers and Booksellers Association) added the Friedenspreis des Deutschen Buchhandels, or Peace Prize, to the activities surrounding the Fair. Typically awarded at the Paulskirche on the final day of the Buchmesse (which itself moved to the Messe site in 1951), the prize is one tool in the Fair's self-construction as a site not merely of international commerce, but of cosmopolitan discourse and the values of intercultural communication. It is awarded to an individual whose work has 'promot[ed] international tolerance' and 'contributed to the . . . ideals' of 'peace, humanity and understanding among all peoples and nations of the world' (Friedenspreis des Deutschen Buchhandels, n.d.).

Such self-constructions by the Buchmesse and those closely connected to it, however, have been problematised. In the late 1960s, when revolutionary protest affected day-to-day life around the world, the Fair's operations were also disrupted. In 1967 publishers joined students in signing an anti-conglomerate declaration against the publisher Springer (which owned the tabloid newspaper *Bild*) on the grounds that too much power in one media group was dangerous (Seyer 2007, 180). In 1968 the organisers of the Buchmesse anticipated further trouble, particularly after the uprisings of the Prague Spring led to the heavy police presence of the 'Polizeimesse' (Police Fair).[15] As it transpired, tensions focused on the award of the Peace Prize to

---

[15] DW includes a photo of this in the gallery '70 Years of the Frankfurt Book Fair', noting in its caption that '1968 went down in Frankfurt's history as the "Police

Senegalese president Léopold Sédar Senghor. Entrances to the Fair were closed in order to prevent attendance, which angered many visitors and exhibitors (Seyer 2007, 205). 'House rules' ('Hausordnung') were introduced, allowing the organisers to close the Fair to the public if the peace ('Messefrieden') was threatened. Police were brought into the Fair and placed on standby with water cannons; events were only allowed with written approval of the Fair (including receptions, press conferences and musical performances). The distribution of posters and leaflets without prior written consent was also banned, alongside the selling of books and other items to visitors (Seyer 2007, 197). The route to an event celebrating the publication of a book by the German finance minister was blocked by protestors, with the latter making fun of the demand to let the police through with the words 'Macht aus Polizisten gute Sozialisten' ('Turn policemen into good socialists'). Some publishers reacted angrily to the Fair's authoritarianism and threatened to stay away the following year if the 'Herr im Haus' ('King of the Castle') approach from the Buchmesse continued. A counter event was held in 1969 (Seyer 2007, 209, 206), with other Gegenbuchmessen in the 1970s and 1980s, as related in Chapter 2.

Meanwhile the Buchmesse affected a stance of political neutrality, saying that 'all nations were to be welcomed, independently of their governments' (Seyer 2007, 165). Such attempted neutrality was immediately hard to sustain on a regional level, given the political tensions between capitalist West Germany and communist East Germany during the Cold War. Which East German publishers were allowed to exhibit was political, not neutral.

The events and activities around 1967–9, then, could readily be viewed as carnivalesque in their questioning of power, upending of (developing) conventions and recuperation of modes of protest through control over (for example) which flags could be flown. While the preceding section might seem an unexpected historical dérive for a book focused primarily on the Fair from 2017 to 2019, the legacy of this carnivalesque period continued into the twenty-first century, including a code of conduct developed from

Fair", with police officers blocking the entrance to the exhibition hall' (Mund and Reucher 2019).

the house rules (Frankfurter Buchmesse 2018a) which reserves the organisers' rights to close the Fair to the public and to expel anyone who does not comply with the code.

Indeed Seyer argues that 1968 was a crucial year in the formation of the Fair's political identity. She cites German chancellor Willy Brandt's speech on the opening of the Buchmesse in 1973, which reflected on the events of five years earlier:

> We faced radical misunderstandings of what freedom of the Fair (Messefreiheit) meant – a misunderstanding that resulted from a long history of mistaking indolence for tolerance, a pseudo-liberal self-satisfaction for democratic self-confidence, intellectual bustle for mental vigour, liberal pathos for the courage to practise real freedom. The Book Fair survived this. It has become an international institution of social life in Germany. (Brandt, quoted in Seyer 2007, 224)

Brandt pitches the Fair as struggling with, then transcending, political and economic turmoil. 'Pseudo-liberal self-satisfaction', or, in the original German 'pseudoliberaler Selbstzufriedenheit', is a term that connotes self-centredness and smugness. It was, in Brandt's account, for too long a part of the Fair's identity; pseudo-liberal self-satisfaction and other undesirable qualities (indolence, bustle, pathos) were confused with genuine intellectual leadership. For Brandt such confusions had receded to the past. But rather than seeing the revolutionary years around 1968 as an interruption to business as usual, Seyer argues that they were crucial to the formation of the Fair's political identity. Because of, rather than despite, these events of 1968, the Buchmesse became a highly visible arena in which to observe the political and economic clashes which shape publishing systems. Surveying the Buchmesse fifty years on from 1968, it is clear that its status as 'an international institution of social life of Germany', in Brandt's words, continues. By examining the political challenges of the late 1960s in more detail, however, we seek to elucidate the political positioning of the Fair. The Fair's 'pseudo-liberal self-satisfaction', if applied to its present-day activities, enables an analysis of the dual role of the Buchmesse in both international business and the formation of cultural-political identity, as the next section reveals.

The Buchmesse and Politics in the Current Juergen

So how does politics intersect with international business within the contemporary Buchmesse? Examining the guest of honour countries provides a route into this discussion, as the same reinforcement of uneven regional power hierarchies is evident in the designation today as with the earlier examples of India and Ireland.

The Buchmesse provides the hall in which the guest of honour exhibits, but other costs associated with hall design and production are borne by the country's agencies and/or government, assisted by any external sponsorship. The act of enabling one country to showcase itself as the Fair's guest of honour is a conferral which operates bidirectionally: the country (at its own cost) reaches extended markets and audiences, but the Buchmesse also derives value: first, from being able to demonstrate the increased commerce which takes place as a direct result of the Fair, and second, through a visible commitment to cosmopolitan discourse (Norrick-Rühl 2020).

And yet, inevitably, the act of showcasing is not neutral; in fact, it has often been a flashpoint for political tension. The designation for Catalonia in 2007 was controversial given the contested state of the region, the prior suppression of its language and culture under the dictatorship of Franco from 1939 to 1975 and its increasingly loud call for independence from Spain. Playing on George Orwell's book title the German newspaper *Spiegel* called it a 'Controversial Homage' (Knapp 2007). Knapp also looked ahead to the subsequent years of 2008 and 2009, when Turkey and China were set to be the guests of honour, both countries which operate oppressive regimes including censorship of the literary and publishing sector. These decisions, in which an aspiration to separate culture from regime, or to encourage a democratic opening out through the means of culture, have been broadly discussed and frequently challenged (Flood 2008; Höbel and Lorenz 2009). These sets of decisions and circumstances suggest that the Buchmesse still operates in a state of political and cultural confusion in which, in Brandt's words, 'real freedom', 'democratic self-confidence', 'intellectual bustle' and 'pseudo-liberal self-satisfaction' sit uncomfortably side by side (Brandt, quoted in Seyer 2007, 224).

The current Juergen (our term for the period since 2005, during which the Buchmesse has been directed by Juergen Boo[k]s) has not been able to cast aside this 'confusion'. In the three years during which we conducted our fieldwork the growing strength of far-right politics across the world, including in Germany, presented challenges to the Fair. In 2017 a meeting we were having in Hall 4 was interrupted by shouting and running; a fight had broken out at the stand of a far-right publisher, one of a series of disturbances occasioned by its presence. The Fair's 'free speech' position was heavily debated as a consequence (*Der Tagesspiegel 2017*). Our novella *The Frankfurt Kabuff* drew on this experience in its construction of its villains, as neo-Nazi publisher and paramilitary group White Storm jeopardise the Buchmesse. The chain of command goes (nearly) to the top, with the Vice President for Intellectual Freedom threatening to bomb the Fair and destroy its intercultural activities:

> There will be NO MORE exchange of ideas! There will be no more translations! No more co-published editions! (Squiscoll 2019a, 66)

The intentional exaggeration of the thriller uses satire to make its analytical point: that there is an inherent and irreconcilable contradiction between the 'On the Same Page' celebration in 2018 of the seventieth anniversary of the Universal Declaration of Human Rights by the Buchmesse and the German Publishers and Booksellers Association, and the admittance of far-right publishers and politicians to the Fair. Neutrality is impossible under such circumstances. The decision to give a platform or not problematises any glib assertion of freedom of speech. So when the director of the Buchmesse made the following statement within the 'On the Same Page' press release, the juxtaposition of discourse and Fair floor reality was striking:

> The Frankfurter Buchmesse brings together hundreds of
> thousands of people from every part of the world.
> Together with political institutions, media partners and
> members of our industry, we want to set an example of
> a peaceful meeting of cultures, thereby making it clear that
> the Frankfurter Buchmesse platform, this 'stage for world
> affairs', only works because basic liberal principles and
> respect for the other are considered non-negotiable values
> here. (Frankfurter Buchmesse 2018b)

The press release's language and the representational discourse of the Fair
demonstrate a continuing pseudo-liberal – or perhaps by 2018 neoliberal –
self-satisfaction or even collective complacency in the mediatised attempt to
contain challenging geopolitics within the commercial and cultural activities
of the Fair.

Publics, Play and Policing

Whose Fair is it anyway? An argument about the Buchmesse's role in brokering
bestsellers, in the international exchange of rights, in enabling the building of
knowledge and networks across the global industry, in hosting publishing's
biggest annual party (albeit smaller than in previous years), in setting the
direction of discussions about human rights and freedom of speech, and in
problematising neoliberal self-satisfaction and complacency suggests the polyvalent nature of the Fair, even to its attendees. Lewis-Kraus discusses the debates
around Turkey as the 2008 guest of honour in 'The Last Book Party', and
usefully brings in the broader publics who live their lives adjacent to the Fair:

> Later in the Fair, Orhan Pamuk will blast the Turkish
> government for its repression of writers ... One night,
> too late and too late in the week, I'll ask some Turks at
> a kebab stand what they think of being the Ehrengast [guest
> of honour country] and what they think of what Pamuk
> says, and they will say that it's good Pamuk is famous but
> why does he have to say all of those things about Armenia.
> (Lewis-Kraus 2009, 49)

The struggle for control over national identity and politics spills out over the bounds of the Messe site in this account. Our own encounters with the wider population of Frankfurt suggested different modes and levels of engagement with the annual event. A Turkish taxi driver pitched a book to a colleague of ours (providing a detail for a crucial plot point in *The Frankfurt Kabuff*); hotel and restaurant staff stood ready for the influx of publishers; shoe shop owners caught some additional trade for their lines of comfortable yet stylish shoes. Frankfurt's famous equine inhabitant Jenny the Horse, on the other hand, took her quotidian walk unbothered by discussion of bestsellers, and end-of-the week drinkers at Yok Yok City Kiosk talked to us about their (lack of) attendance at the Buchmesse (Sanders 2019). Late one night in the Sachsenhausen district the lead singer of a 1990s cover band yelled, 'Is there anybody here from the Book Fair?' Nearly every hand in the crowd went up.

The public is invited into the Buchmesse at the weekend through cheaper ticketing prices, and the German halls are ready for the onslaught, although until 2019 the Fair's rules meant the publishers were only allowed to sell books and other products on Sunday. Public attendance is growing at the Fair (even as other aspects of the Fair contract): from 2018 to 2019 visitor numbers increased by 1 per cent on trade days and by 9.2 per cent on weekend days (*The Bookseller* 2019). An additional draw for the public since 2002 has been the addition of a cosplay area, also discussed in Chapter 2. Incorporating the carnivalesque aspect of cosplay (Winge 2006) into the Fair's commercial fabric draws in new attendees. Costumed adults, teens and children step off trains, into the Hautbahnhof and over to the Buchmesse site dressed as their favourite characters from books, film, TV and anime. The extravagance of the costume and character play might seem removed from the more traditional bookish behaviour and business across the Buchmesse, but bringing it into the Fair is an act of clever programming that is attentive to cross-media flows, global cultural trends and the possibility of further commodification.

Security checkpoints at each entrance to the Buchmesse conduct bag searches. As well as checking whether cosplay swords were props or real weapons (given the threats of global terrorism that have affected German cities and public events), security carefully searched our bags for merchandise we might be bringing into the Fair. Ten copies of *The Frankfurt Kabuff* were deemed a suspiciously commercial amount, but we managed to persuade security to let them through, gifting the young female security guard a copy in return. This search was about safety but, we realised, also about the policing of the Fair's house rules and commercial policies.

The Fair's staff circulate among the halls, ensuring that exhibitors conform to those rules. *Polizei* roam the halls in twos, a little like animals about to board the Ark, watching out for safety issues and occasionally examining the new products of the publishing industry.

Who, then, is in charge of the Fair, what values do they represent, and how might Ullapoolists react to these structures of power and performative display? We venture a response in what follows.

The Frankfurt School, the Situationists and Ullapoolist Interventions (Actual and Non-actualised)

The first year we attended the Buchmesse as Ullapoolist scholar-participants, we prepared ourselves by thinking about the oddity that the biggest annual event of the global book business was located in the city of Frankfurt, sometime home of the Frankfurt School. Two of that school's leading theorists, Horkheimer and Adorno ((1944) 2006), conceptualise the culture industry's production as a capitalist deception of the masses, critical theory that preceded the situationists' later critique of the society of the spectacle. What, we wondered, would the Frankfurt School make of the hyper-commercialisation of (book) culture represented by the bestseller-seeking, international copyright–trading Frankfurter Buchmesse?

We weren't quite sure, though we thought it probably wouldn't be positive. In order to test this idea we put through a small order (two) of custom tote bags to take with us on our first period of fieldwork. We designed 'FRANK/FURT/SCHOOL' across three horizontal lines, reddening the first letter of each (like hand-inked first letters in the early days of Gutenberg's printing) so that the vertical lines read 'FFS' (see Figure 10).

The bags turned out to be conversation starters that could be read in two ways. On one hand, FFS to the astonishing oversupply of books revealed at

Figure 10 Custom FFS tote, with non-actualised boilersuit

the Fair. (We also thought about printing stickers indicating which books we thought superfluous to requirements, but decided against this due to previous professional experience of sticky residue, and because exhibitors probably would not have received it favourably.) On the other hand, FFS to curmudgeonly male theorists who associate a negative vision of mass culture – a category that would include widely read bestsellers – with women, perpetuating gender-based discrimination (see Driscoll 2019 for more).

Our fieldwork in 2017 was guided by such thinking, as well as our search for buzz. Along the way, though, we discovered the gender and racial politics outlined in this chapter. In 2018 we pursued creative investigations in mood, measuring and Kabuff ingress, taking on the personae of journalists Penny Powers and Polly Pringle in order to scrutinise the Fair from the perspective of its official narratives, and writing creative ficto-ethnography in *The Frankfurt Kabuff*. We reacted as Ullapoolists to those structures of power and performative display detailed earlier in this chapter through various interventions, including the Sleaze-O-Meter. For 2019 we originally planned a year of 'full performative' behaviour, wearing red boiler-suits and stiletto heels, musing about burning the Buchmesse down.

These carnivalesque interventions – actual and non-actualised, one-of-a-kind interactive experiences – progressively led us to interrogate our own roles as researchers at the Buchmesse. We came – as to any carnival – to join the fun, as well as to analyse the role of the Fair in the generation of international bestsellers and its place as the fabled centre of global book buzzness. We initially conceptualised our role as Nunu Otots, the insider-outsider figures who cast light on patterns of inclusion and exclusion, in parties as in geopolitics. But we also started to ask ourselves what carnivalesque interventions by scholar-participants might look like, guided by our developing epistemology of Ullapoolism. Although our responses were partly informed by Guy Debord's conceptualisation of the society of the spectacle and methodologically underpinned by the situationists' methods of détournement and dérive, we also enjoyed the parties, revelled in hearing about the trends of the publishing industry and its forthcoming hot titles, and benefited from being at the centre of the book world.

Is this, then, our own neoliberal complacency?

Our research methods tested the carnivalesque narrative about the Buchmesse and its most buzzworthy, bestselling books, and the potential for research both to disrupt and to enable understanding of the book industry and book cultures. Although in the end our approach has not achieved full revolutionary status, its potential is still apparent both in epistemological and in activist terms. The Frankfurter Buchmesse in its carnivalesque nature is literally far from everyday life. And yet immersing ourselves in, analysing and Ullapoolising its acts and effects has led us to conclusions, as the final chapter of this book reveals.

Conclusion: The Broom of History

On the train from Frankfurt to Castle Eltz in 2017 we invented and played an Ullapoolist adaptation of the game 'Guess Who'. In this game two players each have a board with twenty-four flippable pictures of people. The aim is to guess which character the other player has selected. In the normal game a series of yes or no questions such as 'Does your person wear glasses?' leads to elimination and eventually to a guess. Our détournement was designed to develop our fieldwork observations of the Buchmesse. Each character was imagined as an attendee at the Fair, and instead of asking questions about appearance, we asked about motivations and behaviours. Sample questions included:

- Is your person cautious about digital innovation?
- Would your person be (over)excited at the prospect of the extremely legendary Canongate party?
- Does your person stay and help pack up the stand at the end of the Fair?

Playing this game was an awkward process, forcing us to confront and reflect on the impressionistic and sometimes even stereotyping aspects of participant observation.[16] At the same time it allowed us as researchers to turn impressions into questions and to articulate our insights into the activity of the Fair, the personal interactions – networking and meetings, emails and party-going – that together produce the international movement of books, including bestsellers.

Frankfurt is a central node in the people-powered networks that move books, and bestsellers most rapidly and extensively of all. The Buchmesse is a space of multiple actions and reactions: a site for the demonstration of digital practices and face-to-face networking; and a testament to the importance of business-to-business communication in generating buzz, managing mood and building industry culture. It is a forum that demonstrates bestsellers as situations. These books are actively created by people and practices and exert wide-ranging influence. The Fair is also a key agent and

---

[16] We explore the challenges of character creation further in 'Experiments with Book Festival People: (Real and Imaginary)' (Driscoll and Squires, 2020b).

manifestation of the neoliberal ecologies of contemporary publishing, exemplifying the dual role of the Buchmesse in both international business and the formation of cultural-political identity.

In this book we have unpacked the discourse that surrounds the Frankfurt Book Fair and excavated its layers, working through its noise, size, contours, depths and temporality. This conclusion summarises the chapters of this book, which have laid out a theory of buzz generation and thus the publishing buzzness, then dug into the underlying physical structures and the even deeper corporate, geopolitical and gender relations that shape the publishing industry and book culture. This conclusion then presents three of the key ideas developed across this book: the role of the Fair in generating positivity and future-oriented momentum, which operates in dynamic tension with the publishing industry's perpetual sense of existential crisis; the neoliberal self-satisfaction of the Buchmesse; and the excess and waste it generates, including excessive buzz and environmental waste. These ideas together demonstrate the tangled pathways – the extensive and intensive networks, nodes and peripheral points, obstacles and detours – negotiated for bestsellers as they work their way towards international markets via Frankfurt.

Chapter 1 tackled head on how buzz is produced at the Frankfurt Book Fair and how this leads to the publishing of international bestsellers. In our model buzz exists in multiple forms: as marketing-ready information about specific book deals (often including both the number of 000s in a deal and the territories into which a book has been sold), the trends sweeping book culture and the health of the industry. Buzz also exists as a softer, lived experience at the Fair. This experiential mode is bound up in gossip, informal chats, individual emails and meetings. Industry newsletters are key instruments in the conversion from soft to hard buzz, gathering piecemeal information from those on the ground as well as press releases and filtering these into top-level stories. In all its forms buzz is interwoven with the different moods present at Frankfurt: high-key excitement, general positivity, tired but still positive, experiencing difficult moments and negativity. These moods and forms of buzz interact to create the advance marketing for books that become bestsellers, an early B2B (business-to-buzznesss, buzzness-to-business) step in the global promotion of bestselling titles.

Chapter 2 investigated the physical spaces of the Buchmesse in order to add granularity to our understanding of how the Fair produces buzz and bestsellers. A combination of dérives and détournements (including the Cardboard Buchmesse and the Publisher's Stand Reversed) produced a number of findings. First, physical structures are communicative devices that reinforce power relations in the publishing industry: multinational publishers have large stands in prominent positions, smaller publishers have lower or no visibility. The arrangement of publishers in the halls of the Buchmesse is political and shapes understanding of the geopolitics of contemporary book culture, as well as the role of its different players: agents, publishers, publishing services providers, Amazon, cosplayers and self-published authors. The hidden or transient sites of the Fair are even more illuminating, revealing losses and absences, stands that used to be there, people taking a break from the exhaustion of display and buzz generation, the travelling foot soldiers who really must wear comfortable shoes in order to maintain productivity in the creation of buzz for their books. These spaces show the invisible work that goes into trying to make a book a success, as well as more of the pessimism and low moods that play off against the discourse of optimism at the Fair.

Chapter 3 investigated the seeming paradox that the Buchmesse is not only a site for intense commercial exchange, but also a carnival of sorts, operating outside the everyday work environments of the global book industry. We examined partying at the Fair as an instantiation of the publishing industry's power structures: the creation of insiders and out-siders, issues of sleaze and harassment, the hierarchies of power constructed through gender, national groupings, stereotypes and racism. In contra-distinction to such problematic sociopolitical aspects, the Buchmesse's elevated discourse about culture is created, performed and commercialised. The politicised aspects of the bestseller as situation emerged in this chapter: bestsellers are high-profile, party-worthy successes that fulfil market aspira-tions while exerting hierarchising muscle. We considered disruptive ele-ments of the Buchmesse's history that complicate its profile as a forum for advancing freedom of speech and other liberal ideals, showing that such rhetoric is not as severed from commerce as might be assumed. This rhetoric operates in close partnership with neoliberal market logics.

All three chapters enacted an Ullapoolist conceptual approach to the Buchmesse using arts-informed interventions, both actual and non-actualised, in order to satirise and understand the Fair playfully and artistically as we situated ourselves as actors in it. Three overarching ideas or themes emerge from the research as a whole: the interplay of optimism and pessimism at the Fair, the pseudo(neo)liberal self-satisfaction of book culture, and excess and waste.

Optimism and Pessimism: The Moods of Publishing

The Frankfurt Book Fair is a forward-looking, essentially hopeful entity in contemporary book culture: its *raison d'être*, overarching philosophy and the topic of almost all meetings is the future and how the future can include books and book sales. As Hans Christian Rohr from German publishing house C. Bertelsmann told us: 'This is what you're here for in Frankfurt. It's not about complaining, it's about being optimistic and the future is always bright.' Any company or organisation at the Buchmesse might be the source of a new bestseller or a conduit through which a new bestseller passes. Global megaseller *Fifty Shades of Grey* emerged from fan fiction, self-publishing and a small Australian e-press before being boosted by the Frankfurt Book Fair. Every meeting is a site of possibility.

At the same time every person at the Book Fair has aligned themselves with an older media form – the book – and participates in a rhetoric of resilience, of withstanding change. In a 2019 press conference attended by our alter egos Penny Power and Polly Pringle, Fair director Juergen Books quoted Giuseppe Tomasi di Lampedusa's novel *The Leopard*: 'For everything to stay the same, everything must change.' It's an apt quotation for the contemporary publishing industry, and not just because it comes from a book. There is a tension between the exciting momentum of innovation and new hits, and the tendency of the industry to see itself as a stalwart of an older time endangered by the uncertain future of books and reading. Publishing bestsellers and generating buzz requires an optimism that works in tandem with more pessimistic modes of book culture and the publishing industry.

The Pseudo(Neo)liberal Self-Satisfaction of Book Culture

The global book industry, and the version presented 'in miniature' at the large-scale Frankfurt Buchmesse, presents itself incontestably as a world of commerce. But it is also a crucial site for the understanding, analysis and critique of the industry and for the Fair's self-construction as an idealistic site of cosmopolitan and liberal discourse.

Built literally upon the ruins of Frankfurt's war-time bombing, the Buchmesse became a symbolic location for the reconstruction of post-war democracy, a place in which peace, harmony and intercultural communication were foregrounded and intended to be achieved through the ideation of book-(ish) interchange. And yet, as Chapter 3 demonstrated, such a process was inevitably fraught on a local, national and international scale. The pseudo-liberal self-satisfaction of the 1960s and 1970s created numerous challenges to the Buchmesse's intended mode of neutrality, and in order to control both the physical activity and communicative messages of the Fair its organisers sought to exert control over its spaces. In business terms the process has been startlingly effective as the Fair's importance – and its physical size – grew and grew into the twenty-first century. Despite the general retraction of the global economy and of the book industry more specifically, the Buchmesse retains its preeminent place in the annual publishing calendar.

Frankfurt has become a nexus of book-based discussions, from buzz about future bestsellers to more wide-ranging conversations about books, culture and society. But these conversations have repeatedly been challenged by the impossibility of neutrality and by the inherent conflict between ideals such as the tension between freedom of speech and the locking down of content via copyright. The idealism of the Fair has also been challenged by the enactment of sexist and racist behaviours, harassment and stereotyping, and the continual assertion of the hierarchies of the core-periphery model of the industries of the book. If twentieth-century Buchmesse was a site of pseudo-liberal self-satisfaction, its twenty-first-century iteration is firmly and complacently neoliberal in its politics and practices.

In our guise of participant observers at the Frankfurter Buchmesse we also discovered our own neoliberal complacency or, in other words, our compromised position as researchers benefiting from and enjoying conducting research on this global book culture event, even as we commented critically upon some of its practices, behaviours and excesses. Although we dreamed up a fiery end to the Buchmesse – a revolutionary and yet dystopian act ('the image of fire in carnival', Bakhtin writes, is 'deeply ambivalent', 'a fire that simultaneously destroys and renews the world' (Bakhtin 1984, 126)) – we quickly dismissed the thought experiment. Our mode – as the next section admits in its discussion of excess and waste – instead remains one of working within and yet critically commenting upon the industry. This is the position of Ullapoolism, not one of destruction but one in which we look for ways to make contemporary book cultures more progressive, fairer and potentially emancipatory (Driscoll and Squires 2020b).

Excess and Waste

A theme that has run through this book and that we wish to emphasise in this conclusion is that the Frankfurt Book Fair is a site of excess. This can be positive: an overflow of exuberance, an impression of enormity, an abundance of books and people and ideas. In commercial terms the Fair's optimism cannot be matched by the ensuing reality – not every buzzed-about book will become an actual bestseller. The disappointing sales of a hyped book are taken in the stride of an industry that has always been based on calculated risk; annual lists are even created for under-recognised titles. The excess of book buzz in no way diminishes the Frankfurt Book Fair's importance as a creative and generative site for the book business.

Other excesses of the Fair, though, are negative. A sense of waste and dissipation attends the industry both within the physical structures of the Fair and in the global industry it represents. Staff are laid off as companies contract and outsource – they become excess to requirements, and if they are still present they are hustling as contractors in the increasingly fragmented, atomised work culture of the publishing industry (Ray Murray and Squires 2013). An excess of alcohol, licentiousness and opportunities for bad behaviour can lead to harassment. An excess of physical material impedes the sustainability of the industry: stand components are thrown into skips, books are discarded, carpets are torn up. The carbon emitted from planes flying in and out of Frankfurt contributes to climate change and excessive temperatures; we have contributed to these issues ourselves in our fieldwork journeys to and from the Buchmesse. When will the publishing industry – and its researchers, including ourselves – discard its environmentally as well as socially harmful behaviours, migrations and methods? To what extent does the situated knowledge Ullapoolism produces, in its revelation of the complex human and physical dimensions of the paper trails and book circulations of the global book industry, also rely on excess?

Don't discard this book, though. What should you take from it as its overall message? One of the inspirations for our research has been 'low theory', which appeals to us as, in Halberstam's words, 'a counterhegemonic form of theorizing, the theorization of alternatives within an undisciplined zone of knowledge production' (Halberstam 2011, 18). Our research has theorised alternative ways of understanding the role of the Frankfurt Book Fair in the contemporary publishing industry and book cultures, including its role in facilitating the success of bestsellers. In order to succeed commercially and culturally, bestsellers draw on deep and broad social networks within the publishing industry, which are crystallised at the Fair in festive guise. Other things are crystallised at the Fair too, and these turn out to be just as important in determining the shape of publishing and book culture: political debate and uneven geopolitical power relations; conglomerate and behavioural megativity, hierarchisation, gaps and silences; liberal discourse and neoliberal market logics; gender and race-based harassment; a complex choreography of overt visual messaging and traversed, hidden pathways. These layers, these paper trails, assemble and overlap to create the Frankfurter Buchmesse: both a physical mechanism and a symbolic placeholder for the aspirations of contemporary book culture.

***

It's Sunday. The last publisher leaves the Buchmesse as the siren sounds, plane ticket in hand. Paper flutters through the air, words tumbling downwards, curling on the floor. A sound of ripping, hammering, tearing and crashing rings through the halls. Skips are laden to the top with stand fittings, carpet, bunting, books and plastic cups. A *Hausmeister* sweeps the floor, cuttings from trade journals catching in his broom. A small piece of red film catches his eye and he kneels down to pick up a cellophane fish, which he pockets. And as the early evening sun warms his route home, an autumn bee flies across his path.

Acknowledgements

We are tremendously grateful to all the Frankfurt Book Fair attendees who agreed to be interviewed and quoted in this book, and to those who generously spent time with us, invited us to parties and meetings, offered us coffee or the use of power points to charge our phones, and in myriad other ways supported the research for this book. Thank you to Cambridge University Press staff, including Bethany Thomas and Annie Toynbee, Publishing and Book Culture Element series editors Samantha Rayner, Bex Lyons and Leah Tether, Bestsellers thread editors Kim Wilkins, Lisa Fletcher and one of us, Beth Driscoll, and the anonymous peer reviewers for their support in developing this book. We gratefully acknowledge research assistance provided by Sandra van Lente, who sourced and translated the German scholarship and media articles used in this book, and Alexandra Dane, who collected the #fbm19 tweets for analysis. We are also grateful to Geoff Driscoll Architects Pty Ltd, who provided materials and technical expertise in support of the Cardboard Buchmesse; our colleague Kim Wilkins, who participated in 2018 fieldwork with us and co-wrote early sections of *The Frankfurt Kabuff*; and Doris Ruth Eikhof for additional interpretation and German language advice. We acknowledge the input of all those who played with and commented on the Cardboard Buchmesse, early readers of *The Frankfurt Kabuff* on Wattpad, those who made and flew paper planes with us, and those who gave feedback on conference papers related to this research. Some of the ideas in this book appeared in earlier versions in *Post45*, *Interscript*, *Sydney Review of Books*, *Angelaki* and *Mémoires du Livre/Studies in Book Culture*. Funding to support this research was provided by the Australian Research Council Discovery Project DP160101308 'Genre Worlds: Australian Popular Fiction in the Twenty-First Century' and the University of Stirling.

References

Altenhein, Hans, and Stephan Füssel. 2007. *Die Politisierung des Buchmarkts: 1968 als Branchenereignis : Hans Altenhein zum 80. Geburtstag gewidmet*. Mainzer Studien zur Buchwissenschaft, Bd. 15. Wiesbaden: Harrassowitz.

Amaliyar, Subhash, and Gita Wolf. 2015. *Visit the Bhil Carnival*. Tara Books, Chennai.

Appadurai, Arjun. 1986. *The Social Life of Things: Commodities in Cultural Perspective*. Cambridge: Cambridge University Press.

Arcordia, Charles, and Michelle Whitford. 2006. 'Festival Attendance and the Development of Social Capital'. *Journal of Convention & Event Tourism* 8 (2): 1–18. https://doi.org/10.1300/J452v08n02_01

Australian Publishers Association. 2018. 'Farewell Frankfurt for 2018'. www.publishers.asn.au/news/farewell-frankfurt-for-2018

Bakhtin, Mikhail M. 1984. *Problems of Dostoevsky's Poetics*. Translated by Caryl Emerson. Minneapolis: University of Minnesota Press.

Bent, Horace. 2019. "Bent's Notes." *The Bookseller*, October 17, 2019. p. 10.

Bloom, Clive. 2002. *Bestsellers: Popular Fiction since 1900*. Houndmills, Basingstoke.

Books+Publishing. 2017. 'Over Half of Book-Industry Survey Respondents Report Sexual Harassment | Books+Publishing'. *Books+Publishing*. 12 December. www.booksandpublishing.com.au/articles/2017/12/12/99463/over-half-of-book-industry-survey-respondents-report-sexual-harassment/

The Bookseller. 2019. 'Attendance up at Frankfurt Book Fair'. *The Bookseller*. 21 October. www.thebookseller.com/news/attendance-frankfurt-book-fair-1101991

Bourdieu, Pierre. 1993. *The Field of Cultural Production: Essays on Art and Literature*. Cambridge: Polity Press.

Boyle, Karen. 2019. *#MeToo, Weinstein and Feminism*. Cham, Switzerland: Palgrave Pivot.

Brouillette, Sarah. 2007. *Postcolonial Writers in the Global Literary Marketplace*. Basingstoke: Palgrave Macmillan.

Carl, Walter J. 2006. 'What's All the Buzz About? Everyday Communication and the Relational Basis of Word-of-Mouth and Buzz Marketing Practices'. *Management Communication Quarterly* 19 (4): 601–34. https://doi.org/10.1177/0893318905284763

Casanova, Pascale. 2004. *The World Republic of Letters*. Cambridge, MA: Harvard University Press.

Chambers, Claire. 2010. 'Multi-culti Nancy Mitfords and Halal Novelists: The Politics of Marketing Muslim Writers in the UK'. *Textus: English Studies in Italy* 23 (2): 389–403.

Clement, Michel, Dennis Proppe and Armin Rott. 2007. 'Do Critics Make Bestsellers? Opinion Leaders and the Success of Books'. *Journal of Media Economics* 20 (2): 77–105. https://doi.org/10.1080/08997760701193720

Cobb, Shelley, and Tanya Horeck. 2018. 'Post Weinstein: Gendered Power and Harassment in the Media Industries'. *Feminist Media Studies* 18 (3): 489–91. https://doi.org/10.1080/14680777.2018.1456155

Coen, Thérèse. 2017. '7 Tips for Success at Frankfurt Book Fair'. BookMachine. 27 September. https://bookmachine.org/2017/09/27/7-tips-success-frankfurt/

Creative Scotland. 2018. 'Flying the Flag for Scottish Books at Frankfurt Book Fair 2018 | Creative Scotland'. 2018. www.creativescotland.com/explore/read/stories/literature-and-publishing/2018/flying-the-flag-for-scottish-books-at-frankfurt-book-fair-2018

Darnton, Robert. 1982. 'What Is the History of Books?' *Daedalus* 111 (3): 65–83.

Deahl, Rachel, John Maher and Jim Milliot. 2017. 'The Women of Publishing Say #MeToo'. *Publishers Weekly*. 20 October. www.pub lishersweekly.com/pw/by-topic/industry-news/publisher-news/article/75175-sexual-harassment-is-a-problem-in-publishing.html

Debord, Guy. (1967) 2014. *The Society of the Spectacle*. Translated by Ken Knabb. Berkeley: Bureau of Public Secrets.

Der Tagesspiegel. 2017. 'Tumulte bei Höcke-Auftritt auf der Buchmesse'. 15 October. www.tagesspiegel.de/kultur/frankfurter-buchmesse-tumulte-bei-hoecke-auftritt-auf-der-buchmesse/20456380.html

Driscoll, Beth. 2014. *The New Literary Middlebrow: Tastemakers and Reading in the Twenty-First Century*. Basingstoke: Palgrave Macmillan.

    2019. 'Take Bookish Action!' *Sydney Review of Books*. 17 March. https://sydneyreviewofbooks.com/take-bookish-action/

Driscoll, Beth, and DeNel Rehberg Sedo. 2019. 'Faraway, So Close: Seeing the Intimacy in Goodreads Reviews'. *Qualitative Inquiry* 25 (3): 248–59.

Driscoll, Beth, and Claire Squires. 2018a. 'Janelle Monáe or Gerald Murnane?' https://goo.gl/forms/BCncQQrQ7hzZoIu03.

    2018b. 'Serious Fun: Gaming the Book Festival'. *Mémoires Du Livre / Studies in Book Culture* 9 (2). www.erudit.org/en/journals/memoires/2018-v9-n2-memoires03728/1046988ar/

    2018c. '"Oh Look, a Ferry"; or The Smell of Paper Books'. The Lifted Brow. 24 October. www.theliftedbrow.com/liftedbrow/2018/10/24/oh-look-a-ferry-or-the-smell-of-paper-books-by-beth-driscoll-and-claire-squires.

    2020a. 'Experiments with Book Festival People: (Real and Imaginary)'. *Mémoires Du Livre / Studies in Book Culture* 11 (2). www.erudit.org/en/journals/memoires/2020-v11-n2-memoires05373/1070271ar/

    2020b. 'The Epistemology of Ullapoolism: Making Mischief from within Contemporary Book Cultures (Forthcoming)'. *Angelaki* 25 (5).

2020c. 'Megativity and Miniaturization at the Frankfurt Book Fair'. Post45: Ecologies of Neoliberal Publishing. 8 April. http://post45.org/2020/04/megativity-and-miniaturization-at-the-frankfurt-book-fair/

DW. 2006. 'Small Publishers Squeeze Together at Frankfurt Book Fair'. DW.COM. www.dw.com/en/small-publishers-squeeze-together-at-frankfurt-book-fair/a-2195706

Ellmann, Lucy. 2019. *Ducks, Newburyport*. Norwich: Galley Beggar Press.

Escarpit, Robert. 1966. *The Book Revolution*. Harrap.

Ewen, Paul. 2014. *Francis Plug: How to Be a Public Author*. Norwich: Galley Beggar Press.

Fiegerman, Seth. 2018. 'The Typical Amazon Employee Makes Less than You Think'. CNNMoney. 19 April. https://money.cnn.com/2018/04/19/technology/amazon-employee-salary/index.html

Flood, Alison. 2008. 'Will Frankfurt Open Turkey's Censored Books?' *The Guardian*. 16 October. www.theguardian.com/books/2008/oct/16/book-fair-turkey-censorship-frankfurt

2015. 'How Amazon Came to Dominate Fiction in Translation'. *The Guardian*. 9 December. www.theguardian.com/books/2015/dec/09/amazon-publishing-translated-fiction-amazoncrossing-sales

2018. '"Up-Lit" Gives Hope to Publishers at Frankfurt Book Fair'. *The Guardian*. 12 October. www.theguardian.com/books/2018/oct/12/up-lit-gives-hope-to-publishers-at-frankfurt-book-fair

Frankfurter Buchmesse. 2018a. 'Hausordnung Der Frankfurter Buchmesse'. www.buchmesse.de/files/media/pdf/service-hausordnung-frankfurter-buchmesse.pdf

2018b. 'On The Same Page'. 8 August. www.buchmesse.de/en/press/press-releases/2018-08-08-onthesamepage

2019a. 'Get to Know Frankfurter Buchmesse'. www.buchmesse.de/en/about-us

2019b. 'The Business Hub of Frankfurter Buchmesse'. www.buchmesse .de/en/exhibit/collective-exhibitions/business-hub

2019c. 'The Cosplay Area of Frankfurter Buchmesse – the Full Programme'. www.buchmesse.de/en/highlights/cosplay

2019d. 'Business Club Ambassadors'. Accessed 20 December 2019. www .buchmesse.de/en/visit/trade-visitors/business-ticket/ambassador

Friedenspreis des Deutschen Buchhandels. n.d. 'The Statute'. Accessed 25 November 2019. www.friedenspreis-des-deutschen-buchhandels.de/ 445942/

Füssel, Stephan, ed. 1999. *50 Jahre Frankfurter Buchmesse: 1949–1999*. Orig.- Ausg., 1. Aufl. Suhrkamp Taschenbuch 3045. Frankfurt am Main: Suhrkamp.

Garry, Emer. 2017. 'The Frankfurt Book Fair: 5 Tips for First-Time Visitors'. Emer Garry Editing. 18 March. https://emergarryediting .com/2017/03/18/frankfurt-book-fair-tips/

Gelder, Ken. 2004. *Popular Fiction: The Logics and Practices of a Literary Field*. Milton Park, Abingdon, Oxfordshire; New York: Routledge.

Geller, Jonny. 2018. 'My Frankfurt Book Fair . . . with Jonny Geller'. *The Bookseller*. 10 October. www.thebookseller.com/insight/my-frank furt-book-fair-jonny-geller-871971

Gonsalves, Roanna. 2015. 'The Survival of the Friendliest: Contemporary Indian Publishing in English at the Frankfurt Book Fair'. *Cultural Sociology* 9 (3): 425–46. https://doi.org/ 10.1177/1749975515590244.

Gould, Emily. 2007. 'No One Got Naked At the Frankfurt Book Fair This Year'. Gawker. 19 October. http://gawker.com/312820/no-one- got-naked-at-the-frankfurt-book-fair-this-year.

Grindon, Gavin. 2004. 'Carnival against Capital: A Comparison of Bakhtin, Vaneigem and Bey'. *Anarchist Studies* 12 (2): 147–61.

Halberstam, Jack. 2011. *The Queer Art of Failure*. Durham, NC: Duke University Press.

Hardt, Michael. 1999. 'Affective Labor'. *Boundary 2* 26 (2): 89–100.

Hartmann, Markus. 2014. 'Distribution and Money, the Frankfurt Book Fair and the PhotoBookMuseum, Cologne – Still Searching – Fotomuseum Winterthur'. *Fotomuseum* (blog). 10 October. www .fotomuseum.ch/en/explore/still-searching/articles/26993_distribu tion_and_money_the_frankfurt_book_fair_and_the_photobookmu seum_cologne

Hertwig, Luise. 2020. 'State-Funded Support of International Trade in Rights and Licences: Translation Funding Programs of Guests of Honor Argentina and France at the 2010 and 2017 Frankfurt Book Fair'. *Mémoires Du Livre / Studies in Book Culture* 11 (2). www.erudit.org/en/journals/memoires/2020-v11-n2-mem oires05373/1070264ar/

Hessenchau. 2019. 'Buchmesse-Infos: +++ Kehraus in den Messehallen, Buchmesse knackt 300.000er-Marke, Atwood setzt auf Greta +++'. hessenschau.de. 20 October. www.hessenschau.de/kultur/buch messe/buchmesse-infos–kehraus-in-den-messehallen-buchmesse- knackt-300000er-marke-atwood-setzt-auf-greta–,ticker-buchmesse- sonntag-100.html

Highmore, Ben. 2013. 'Feeling Our Way: Mood and Cultural Studies'. *Communication and Critical/Cultural Studies* 10 (4): 427–38. https:// doi.org/10.1080/14791420.2013.840387

Höbel, Wolfgang, and Andreas Lorenz. 2009. 'China, the Unwelcome Guest: Controversy as Frankfurt Book Fair Fetes Beijing'. *Spiegel Online*. 13 October. www.spiegel.de/international/world/china-the- unwelcome-guest-controversy-as-frankfurt-book-fair-fetes-beijing- a-654713.html

Horkheimer, Max, and Theodor W. Adorno. (1944) 2006.'The Culture Industry: Enlightenment As Mass Deception'. In *Media and Cultural Studies: Keywords*, edited by Meenakshi Gigi Durham and Douglas M. Kellner, 41–72. Malden, MA: Blackwell.

Huggan, Graham. 2001. *The Postcolonial Exotic: Marketing the Margins*. New York: Routledge.

John Sutherland. 1978. *Fiction and the Fiction Industry*. London: The Athlone Press.

Kirschenbaum, Matthew, and Sarah Werner. 2014. 'Digital Scholarship and Digital Studies: The State of the Discipline'. *Book History* 17 (1): 406–58. https://doi.org/10.1353/bh.2014.0005

Knapp, Margit. 2007. 'A Controversial Homage to Catalonia: Commerce Replaces Politics at the Frankfurt Book Fair'. *Spiegel Online*. 9 October. www.spiegel.de/international/germany/a-controversial-homage-to-catalonia-commerce-replaces-politics-at-the-frankfurt-book-fair-a-510291.html

Lewis-Kraus, Gideon. 2009. 'The Last Book Party'. *Harper's*. March. https://harpers.org/archive/2009/03/the-last-book-party/5/

Mansfield, Katie. 2019. 'Non-fiction Leads the Way As Climate Titles Dominate Discussion at Frankfurt'. *The Bookseller*. 18 October. www.thebookseller.com/news/non-fiction-leads-way-climate-titles-dominate-discussion-frankfurt-1100876

Mautref, Jessica. 2018. '11 Tips for the 2018 Frankfurt Book Fair'. https://blog.gutenberg-technology.com/en/10-tips-2018-frankfurt-book-fair

Miller, Laura J. 2000. 'The Best-Seller List As Marketing Tool and Historical Fiction'. *Book History* 3 (1): 286–304. https://doi.org/10.1353/bh.2000.0012

Moeran, Brian. 2010. 'The Book Fair As a Tournament of Values'. *Journal of the Royal Anthropological Institute* 16 (1): 138–54. https://doi.org/10.1111/j.1467–9655.2009.01601.x

2011. 'Trade Fairs, Markets and Fields: Framing Imagined As Real Communities'. *Messen, Märkte Und Felder: Die Rahmung von Imaginierten Als Reale Gemeinschaften von Marktteilnehmern.* 36 (3): 79–98.

Morris, Linda. 2018. 'Nevermoor Wins Independent Booksellers' Book of the Year'. *Sydney Morning Herald*. 26 March. www.smh.com.au/entertainment/art-and-design/nevermoor-wins-independent-booksellers-book-of-the-year-20180325-p4z65z.html

Mott, Frank Luther. 1947. *Golden Multitudes: The Story of Best Sellers in the United States*. New York: Macmillan.

Mund, Heike, and Gaby Reucher. 2019. '70 Years of the Frankfurt Book Fair'. DW.COM. 14 October. www.dw.com/en/70-years-of-the-frankfurt-book-fair/g-50823052

Murray, Simone. 2012. *The Adaptation Industry: The Cultural Economy of Contemporary Literary Adaptation*. New York: Routledge.

2018. *The Digital Literary Sphere: Reading, Writing, and Selling Books in the Internet Era*. Baltimore, MD: Johns Hopkins University Press.

Nawotka, Ed. 2019a. 'Frankfurt Updates Hall Plan, Adds Audiobook Focus'. *Publishers Weekly*. 3 September. www.publishersweekly.com/pw/by-topic/international/Frankfurt-Book-Fair/article/81077-frankfurt-updates-hall-plan-adds-audiobook-focus.html

2019b. 'Frankfurt Book Fair 2019: Netflix V-P Talks Book Strategy'. *PublishersWeekly.Com*. 17 October. www.publishersweekly.com/pw/by-topic/international/Frankfurt-Book-Fair/article/81493-frankfurt-book-fair-2019-netflix-v-p-talks-book-strategy.html

Niemeier, Sabine. 2001. *Funktionen Der Frankfurter Buchmesse Im Wandel – Von Den Anfangen Bis Heute*. Buchwissenschaftliche Beiträge aus dem Deutschen Bucharchiv München, Bd. 68. Wiesbaden: Harrassowitz.

Norrick-Rühl, Corinna. 2019. *Internationaler Buchmarkt*. Frankfurt: Bramann.

    2020. '"Die Buchwelt Zu Gast in Frankfurt": Understanding the Impact of the Guest of Honour Presentation at Frankfurt Book Fair on the German Literary Marketplace'. *Mémoires Du Livre / Studies in Book Culture* 11 (2). www.erudit.org/en/journals/memoires/2020-v11-n2-memoires05373/1070263ar/

Owen, Lynette. 2019. *Selling Rights*. Abingdon, Oxon, New York: Routledge.

Publishing Scotland. 2019. 'Frankfurt Book Fair: 16 to 20 October 2019'. www.publishingscotland.org/events/frankfurt-book-fair-16-to-20-october-2019/

Rahman, Khaleda. 2018. 'Anna Todd Cancels Talk at Frankfurt Book Fair after Being "Harassed."' *Daily Mail*. 15 October. www.dailymail.co.uk/news/article-6278373/Anna-Todd-cancels-talk-Frankfurt-book-fair-harassed-hours.html

Ray Murray, Padmini, and Claire Squires. 2013. 'The Digital Communications Circuit'. *Book 2.0* 3 (1): 3–24.

Ricchetti, Laura. 2019. 'My Frankfurt Book Fair . . . with Laura Ricchetti'. *The Bookseller*. 16 October.

Richard, Christine. 2006. 'Buchmesse? Nie Wieder! Selbsterfahrungsbericht Aus Dem Gelände Schwallender Verleger, Schwellende Flüsse Und Schwindender Sinne'. *Du: Die Zeitschrift Der Kultur*. www.e-periodica.ch/digbib/view?pid=dkm-003:2006:66::2259#744

Rose, Heather. 2018. 'Heather Rose: My Year of Wonder'. *Sydney Morning Herald*. 14 December. www.smh.com.au/entertainment/art-and-design/heather-rose-my-year-of-wonder-20181212-p50lok.html

Saha, Anamik. 2016. 'The Rationalizing/Racializing Logic of Capital in Cultural Production'. *Media Industries* 3 (1). https://quod.lib.umich.edu/m/mij/15031809.0003.101?view=text;rgn=main

Sanders IV, Lewis. 2019. 'Horse Takes Daily Stroll through Frankfurt – without Owner | DW | 09. 03.2019'. DW.COM. 9 March. www.dw.com/en/horse-takes-daily-stroll-through-frankfurt-without-owner/a-47833431

Sapiro, Gisèle. 2010. 'Globalization and Cultural Diversity in the Book Market: The Case of Literary Translations in the US and in France'. *Poetics* 38 (4): 419–39. https://doi.org/10.1016/j.poetic.2010.05.001

——— 2016. 'The Metamorphosis of Modes of Consecration in the Literary Field: Academies, Literary Prizes, Festivals'. *Poetics* 59: 5–19. https://doi.org/10.1016/j.poetic.2016.01.003

Seyer, Ulrike. 2007. 'Die Frankfurter Buchmesse in den Jahren 1967–1969'. In *Die Politisierung des Buchmarkts: 1968 als Branchenereignis : Hans Altenhein zum 80. Geburtstag gewidmet*, edited by Stephan Füssel, 159–241. Wiesbaden: Harrassowitz.

Snaije, Olivia. 2019. 'Literary Agents Buzz at the 2019 Frankfurt Book Fair'. *Publishing Perspectives*. 16 October. https://publishingperspectives.com/2019/10/rights-buzz-as-2019-frankfurter-buchmesse-opens/.

Squires, Claire. 'Taste and/or Big Data?: Post-Digital Editorial Selection.' *Critical Quarterly* 59, no. 3 (2017): 24–38. https://doi.org/10.1111/criq.12361.

Squires, Claire. 2007. *Marketing Literature: The Making of Contemporary Literature in Britain*. Houndsmills: Palgrave Macmillan.

——— 2020. 'Sensing the Novel-Seeing the Book-Selling the Goods' (forthcoming). In *The Novel as Network*, edited by Corinna Norrick-Rühl and Tim Lazendörfer. Basingstoke: Palgrave Macmillan.

Squires, Claire, and Beth Driscoll. 2018. 'The Sleaze-O-Meter: Sexual Harassment in the Publishing Industry'. *Interscript*. 8 March. www .interscriptjournal.com/online-magazine/sleaze-o-meter

Squiscoll, Blaire. 2019a. *The Frankfurt Kabuff*. Glasgow and Melbourne: Kabuff Books.

2019b. 'The Frankfurt Kabuff Party 1 (Extremely Legendary), a Playlist by Blaire Squiscoll on Spotify'. Spotify. https://open.spotify.com/ playlist/0eXv8z8jZGyJBEWYAZFcNi

Steger, Jason. 2019. 'Bookmarks: The Sound of Adrian McKinty Working on a Chain Gang'. *Sydney Morning Herald*. 19 April. www.smh.com .au/entertainment/books/bookmarks-the-sound-of-adrian-mckinty-working-on-a-chain-gang-20190416-p51ejj.html

Steiner, Ann. 2014. 'Serendipity, Promotion, and Literature: The Contemporary Book Trade and International Megasellers'. In *Hype: Bestsellers and Literary Culture*, edited by Jon Helgason, Sara Kärrholm and Ann Steiner, 55–90. Lund: Nordic Academic Press.

Sullivan, Jane. 2018. 'Turning Pages: Three Cheers for Up Lit'. *Sydney Morning Herald*. 6 December. www.smh.com.au/entertainment/ books/turning-pages-three-cheers-for-up-lit-20181206-h18u2i.html

Sutherland, John. 1981. *Bestsellers: Popular Fiction of the 1970s*. London; Boston: Routledge & Kegan Paul.

2002. *Reading the Decades: Fifty Years of the Nation's Bestselling Books*. London: BBC.

2007. *Bestsellers: A Very Short Introduction*. Very Short Introductions. Oxford, New York: Oxford University Press.

Taylor, D. J. 1989. *A Vain Conceit: British Fiction in the 1980s*. London: Bloomsbury.

Thompson, John B. *Merchants of Culture: The Publishing Business in the Twenty-First Century*. Cambridge: Polity Press, 2010.

Tivnan, Tom. 2018. 'Petition Launched over FBF LitAg Move'. *The Bookseller*. 10 October. www.thebookseller.com/news/petition-launched-over-fbf-litag-move-873716

2019. 'My Frankfurt Book Fair: Mary Darby'. *The Bookseller*. 17 October.

Treglown, Jeremy, and Bridget Bennett, eds. 1998. *Grub Street and the Ivory Tower: Literary Journalism and Literary Scholarship from Fielding to the Internet*. Oxford, New York: Oxford University Press.

Vaneigem, Raoul. 2001. *The Revolution of Everyday Life*. Translated by Donald Nicholson-Smith. Expanded edition. London: Rebel Press.

Weber, Millicent. 2018. *Literary Festivals and Contemporary Book Culture*. New York: Palgrave Macmillan.

Weber, Millicent, and Beth Driscoll. 2019. 'Playful Twitter Accounts and the Socialisation of Literary Institutions'. *First Monday* 24 (3). https://doi.org/10.5210/fm.v24i3.9486

Weidhaas, Peter. 2007. *A History of the Frankfurt Book Fair*. Toronto: Dundurn Press.

2009. 'The Frankfurt Book Fair: 60 Years and Still a Shining Example'. *Publishing Research Quarterly* 25 (1): 30–5. https://doi.org/10.1007/s12109-008–9099-2.

Williams, Sue. 2012. 'The Secret of Global Appeal'. *Sydney Morning Herald*. 19 October. www.smh.com.au/entertainment/books/the-secret-of-global-appeal-20121019-27v4i.html

Winge, Theresa. 2006. 'Costuming the Imagination: Origins of Anime and Manga Cosplay.' *Mechademia* 1 (1): 65–76.

Cambridge Elements ≡

Publishing and Book Culture

SERIES EDITOR

Samantha Rayner
University College London

Samantha Rayner is a Reader in UCL's Department of
Information Studies. She is also Director of UCL's Centre for
Publishing, co-Director of the Bloomsbury CHAPTER
(Communication History, Authorship, Publishing, Textual
Editing and Reading) and co-editor of the Academic Book of
the Future BOOC (Book as Open Online Content) with UCL
Press.

ASSOCIATE EDITOR

Leah Tether
University of Bristol

Leah Tether is Professor of Medieval Literature and Publishing
at the University of Bristol. With an academic background in
medieval French and English literature and a professional
background in trade publishing, Leah has combined her
expertise and developed an international research profile in
book and publishing history from manuscript to digital.

ADVISORY BOARD

Simone Murray, Monash University

Claire Squires, University of Stirling

Andrew Nash, University of London

Leslie Howsam, Ryerson University

David Finkelstein, University of Edinburgh

Alexis Weedon, University of Bedfordshire

Alan Staton, Booksellers Association

Angus Phillips, Oxford International Centre for Publishing

Richard Fisher, Yale University Press

John Maxwell, Simon Fraser University

Shafquat Towheed, The Open University

Jen McCall, Emerald Publishing

About the Series

This series aims to fill the demand for easily accessible, quality texts available for teaching and research in the diverse and dynamic fields of Publishing and Book Culture. Rigorously researched and peer-reviewed Elements will be published under themes, or 'Gatherings'. These Elements should be the first check point for researchers or students working on that area of publishing and book trade history and practice: we hope that, situated so logically at Cambridge University Press, where academic publishing in the UK began, it will develop to create an unrivalled space where these histories and practices can be investigated and preserved.

Cambridge Elements ☰

Publishing and Book Culture
Bestsellers

Gathering Editor: Beth Driscoll
Beth Driscoll is Associate Professor in Publishing and
Communications at the University of Melbourne. She is the author of
The New Literary Middlebrow (Palgrave Macmillan, 2014), and her
research interests include contemporary reading and publishing,
genre fiction and post-digital literary culture.

Gathering Editor: Lisa Fletcher
Lisa Fletcher is Professor of English at the University of
Tasmania. Her books include Historical Romance Fiction:
Heterosexuality and Performativity (Ashgate, 2008) and Popular
Fiction and Spatiality: Reading Genre Settings (Palgrave
Macmillan, 2016).

Gathering Editor: Kim Wilkins
Kim Wilkins is an Associate Professor of Writing and Publishing at
the University of Queensland. She is also the author of more than
thirty popular fiction novels.

ELEMENTS IN THE GATHERING

Printed in the United States
By Bookmasters